Equine Muscle Magic

Dedication

To Shadow

He illuminated my path to the healing art of Equine Massage.

Equine Muscle Magic

A Simple, Easy-to-Use Guide
for Massaging Your Horse

Jackie Nairn

Disclaimer

To horse owners or anyone else who reads this book, the information given is not intended to be taken as a replacement for professional veterinary or medical advice. The information presented in Equine Muscle Magic is intended to be used as complementary therapy alongside the care, treatment and advice provided by your veterinarian. A veterinarian must always be consulted for any concerns or problems whatsoever with an equine. Neither the author nor the publisher can be held responsible for any loss or claim arising out of the use or misuse of the suggestions made in this book, nor the failure to take professional veterinary advice. The reader or user of the information presented in this book assumes the entire responsibility and liability for his or her actions.

Order this book online at www.trafford.com
or email orders@trafford.com

Most Trafford titles are also available at major online book retailers.

ISBN: 978-1-4269-3060-7 (sc)
ISBN: 978-1-4269-3080-5 (dj)

Library of Congress Control Number: 2010904145

Our mission is to efficiently provide the world's finest, most comprehensive book publishing service, enabling every author to experience success. To find out how to publish your book, your way, and have it available worldwide, visit us online at www.trafford.com

Trafford rev. 04/06/2010

 www.trafford.com

North America & international
toll-free: 1 888 232 4444 (USA & Canada)
phone: 250 383 6864 ♦ fax: 812 355 4082

Equine Muscle Magic

Introduction

It's magical how just the simple act of laying your hands on a horse's muscles can bring such dramatic change to both the horse and to you. Massaging and manipulating the muscles can cause profound changes in your horse's health, his performance, and his trust in you. These changes go deep, beyond just the physical act of manipulating the muscles. They bring about physiological changes to the muscles at a cellular level that increase muscle health and performance. And they can induce psychological effects that increase the horse's emotional and mental health.

These tactile interactions can create a "multi-level connection" that will deepen the relationship you have with your horse. And the wonderful thing is that everyone has the ability to achieve this connection and experience the joy that comes with it. You only need to bring the intent to learn and the desire to relate to your horse on a new level. This book will bring you the tools that you need to carry out that intent and to achieve that desire.

I have been pondering writing about massage therapy for horse owners for a very long time. I have been practicing as a professional equine massage therapist for a number of years and have worked on hundreds of horses. Almost without exception, the owners of my equine massage clients want to know what they can do to help maintain their horse's health and performance between professional massage sessions. As a result, "Equine Muscle Magic" has been swimming around in my head for the better part of the past decade.

Through this book, I want to inspire horse owners to use massage as a tool to connect on a deeper, more enriching level with their horses. It will help you to develop and expand the bond that you already have with your horse. It will not only deepen the physical, psychological, and physiological relationship that you have, but also enhance the love and affection felt by both of you.

Once your horse understands that you are giving back to him and addressing his body needs, the connection becomes unlimited. It will grow into a true human/horse relationship, one in which each gives to the other. It may take a little time for your horse to understand that you are there strictly to give to him, to address the needs of his body, and not just to give him shots or to take him out riding. You may only be able to massage him a few moments at a time in the beginning; but as his trust builds, you will find that he will let you do more in every session.

This book is designed to take the guess work out of massaging your horse. It will give you step-by-step instructions for each of the interactions that you will want to perform. It will show you how to give your horse a "10-Minute Massage" for use between full-body massages or when you don't have time for a complete treatment. It will also show you how to build a "body map" of your horse, locating all the places where his muscles are in need of work. And finally, it will provide you with the complete procedure for giving your horse a full-body massage from head to tail.

In addition, the book will show you how to do stretches for both yourself and your horse that will prepare both of you for a safer and more enjoyable ride. It will also take you through some mental exercises to clear your mind and prepare you for approaching the massage with a proper attitude. And finally, it will look at a number of muscle problems that are the result of specific activities (such as trail riding, jumping, dressage, and endurance riding) and show you which muscles are affected and how to relieve their stress.

This is not intended to be a technical anatomy book. It is an easy-to-use, user-friendly guide designed for horse owners to learn how to massage their own horses between professional sessions. There is enough technical information provided to allow non-professionals to achieve significant changes in equine muscle health and performance, while at the same time building a multi-level connection in their human/horse relationship. If you want a technical reference text, you might consider purchasing Dr. Nancy Loving's "All Systems Go" veterinary manual (see the Appendix for a reference).

My goal for "Equine Muscle Magic" is to help as many horses as possible live a healthier, more emotionally-stable life that is filled with love. If I can teach horse owners to achieve this goal with their horses through the proper use of massage, I will feel that I have made my contribution to the equine world that I love.

Imagine how empty our lives would be without horses. I want every horse owner to have the ability to make a significant change in the way their horses live their lives. Horses truly want to be companions of humans. How else can you explain how a 100+ pound human can manage a 1200-pound animal. I believe it is because horses truly want to be with humans and even have a desire to take care of us. It's their immense capacity to love that allows them to be generous toward us humans, even when we exhibit our many flaws. Through the years, horses have helped me through the loss of loved ones and other emotionally trying times, and have helped me celebrate many happy events. Horses have reduced the sting of my tears and helped me celebrate the happiness of living. I am so very grateful that they have graced my life and helped to keep me balanced. It is only fitting that I return the favor to them in any way I can.

Chapter 1:

Growing Up With Horses

Before introducing you to the tools and techniques of equine massage, I want to share with you some of the things I have learned from the many horses that have graced my life. As I mentioned in the introduction, one of the benefits of your learning and practicing massage is to develop a multi-level connection with your horse that will deepen your relationship. Just like people, every horse you interact with will have a singular personality, and require a different approach to get the most out of your relationship. If you learn to recognize the subtle signs that they give you about how they are feeling and how they want to interact with you, you can approach the relationship in a way that will enrich the bond between you and your horse.

In the next few pages, I will portray the personalities of some of the more important horses in my life and what I learned from each of them. I hope that if some of these experiences strike a familiar cord in the relationship you have with your horse, you might come to a better understanding of your horse's personality and how to better interact with him or her.

I have been passionate about horses for over 50 years. The handful of horses I'm sharing with you in this text were all great teachers and added to the person I am today. It was largely through them that I learned self confidence and self reliance. Through loving them

I gained the compassion and caring that I now feel for all living things.

Horses have been a part of human society for many thousands of years. Every country has used horses to help in their commerce and for personal satisfaction and growth. In France the word horse derives from "divine mind and reason". In Greek, Ikkos, the word for horse, means "great light". The Hebrew word for horse means "to explain". Equus, the Latin word for horse, means "light of great mind or soul". The Blackfoot Indians refer to the horse as "medicine elk". And in Europe, Asia, and North America the horse has achieved spiritual significance and a divine status. In some cultures, the horse has been used for purposes of divination, believing the sacred beasts to be in contact with God more than their priests are. In ancient Babylon, they believed the horse to be god or "Zu". It is no wonder that so many of us revere the horse and look to him for healing.

The horse has the ability to heal our souls. Today, horses are used to help humans overcome many physical and mental maladies. Whether they are being used for therapeutic riding or just taking away our pain, horses heal us!

With all that horses present to us, it is only fitting that we give back to them by providing a caring and nourishing environment, along with humane and loving treatment. Whenever we ask them to perform for us – whether it be on the race track, the show arena, or just riding along a pleasure trail – it should be incumbent on us to insure that their physical and emotional well-being needs are nurtured.

One way of doing this is through equine massage. It is one of the simplest and most basic ways to build and nurture your equine's spirit, while at the same time building and nurturing you own.

Whoever said "there is something about the outside of a horse that is good for the inside of a man" was right. They have the ability to take away our sorrow, lift up our heart, and make us glad that we will live another day. Horses act as a catalyst for us, allowing us to sort out our problems. I've owned about 30 horses over my lifetime, and the ones I'm writing about here taught me the most. I believe that each of these horses came into my life to help me grow. They gave me great joy to be with them, and great sorrow when they passed on. But I wouldn't have missed them for the world. I can't imagine living my life without horses.

Chapter 2:

Horses Were My Teachers

For me, it all started on my sixth birthday. My mother took me and some of my friends to Island Grove Park, in Greeley Colorado. One of the attractions there was the pony ride, ubiquitous throughout amusement parks in the 1950's. Here the ponies were tied to a bar in a spoke ring and walked in a circle, providing a fifteen-minute thrill for their eager young riders. For most of these city kids, this was their only experience with a real, live equine. For me, it was where my life-long love affair with horses began.

I don't remember the name of the horse that I got to ride, but I vividly remember his big, kind eyes as he nuzzled my shock of natural-curly hair. He was a beautiful white pony, and from my six-year-old perspective, seemed as big as a house. He had that wonderful "horsy" aroma that to this day I still love to smell in my own horse. I remember touching him and feeling that his coat was like velvet. My memory of the rest of my birthday is only a blur, and my only vivid recollection is riding that horse.

After that, I sought out any opportunity to again get on the back of a horse. There was a man in our neighborhood who owned a horse and would ride by from time to time. I would run out and beg him to let me ride double. He was a kind man, and would allow me to ride with him around the field for hours before finally making me get off.

The thing I wanted most in the world was a horse of my own. As luck would have it, I was an underweight, emaciated child. I didn't find food very interesting; eating was something I had to do, only because my parents insisted. The doctor once actually called my parents in for a discussion because he was concerned that I might be being abused through malnutrition. He thought that because I was the youngest of four children, perhaps my parents didn't have enough money to support us and there wasn't enough food to go around. The truth was that I found life boring and eating just didn't interest me.

The doctor told my parents that they had to find something that I loved enough to use as a bribe to make me eat. As a result, for my seventh birthday, I got my first horse named Arrow. The deal was that if I ate all my meal, then I could go out and be with him. From that time on there have always been horses in my life.

Arrow

My father was a contractor who built custom-designed homes on acreages, which meant we always lived on the edge of town where there was usually room to erect a small shed and a corral for my horse. I learned that my father also had a love for horses as a boy growing up in Nebraska. His father owned a grain mill and a farm where my father could ride a pony that he had been given. My father told me that he would ride his pony, at a full gallop, down the dirt lane to their home and shoot the glass insulators off of the phone poles. That game came to an abrupt end when his father discovered what he had been doing. And it all came to an end when the farm, the grain mill, and that good little pony were all lost during the "Great Depression". But my father never lost his love for horses, and when he decided that he had to get a horse for me, he brought home a wonderful, big bay horse named Arrow.

It was my good fortune that my first horse was an old horse with the "patience of Job". At seven years old, I was so small that I had to stand Arrow by the fence to get him tacked. I would have to keep lugging the saddle up the rails of the fence, one by one, until I could get it even with his back and could fling the saddle over onto him. And all the time he would just stand calmly while I persisted with my struggles. Once I finally got him tacked, by using a combination of a large bucket, the saddle leathers, and the fence rails, I would manage to drag myself on. During all this maneuvering, Arrow would patiently wait until I was securely seated, and only then would he move on.

I truly believe that horses have a sixth sense about caring for humans. Arrow was my guardian. He kept me from getting into trouble, even when I messed things up by trying to fall off. He just waited for me to get straightened out before continuing on. I can remember thinking "I've got wheels; I can go anyplace, and I'm free." From that time on, my parents were relieved of responsibility for me. He was the best babysitter that they could have hired.

It took me quite a while to comprehend what Arrow must have known all along – that learning to ride is a series of baby steps. The life lessons that Arrow taught me were about kindness, patience, and never giving up until you get the proper outcome. He also taught me not to expect rapid results, and to celebrate each progress, even when it comes in small steps.

Domino

It was not too long after Arrow arrived at our home that another horse came to live with us. My father's experience with horses had taught him that they need companionship of their own kind. He decided that my sister, Penny, should also have a horse, perhaps because he thought if my horse kept me out of his hair, it might well work the same for her.

Domino was a handsome black horse of about seven years, with a baled face and white socks. Over the years that we owned him, I totally lost track of the number of times that he stepped on my feet. It seemed like I couldn't walk into his corral without him immediately coming over and standing on one of my feet. I don't know what I ever did to that horse to make him want to do that; or maybe he just liked standing on my feet!

Penny and I had great fun with that horse. During the '50s, everyone thought it was a cool thing to do to teach your horse to rear like "Roy Rogers and Trigger". So we promptly set out to teach Domino to be a real movie horse. After a couple of weeks, we had him rearing on command. Unfortunately, he also thought this was a great trick and used it whenever he wanted to protest something we wanted him to do. We were so proud of our new trick, that we staged a scene where we rode up next to my father and had Domino rear. Needless to say, my father didn't think it was so cool. He was thoroughly disgusted and could have killed us for teaching Domino such a bad habit. I don't think Domino ever did understand why we went to such lengths to get him to unlearn his new trick.

I loved all horses, and just assumed that they felt the same way about me. What I learned from Domino was that no matter how hard you try, some horses just aren't going to like you back. So get over it.

BD Boy

One day when I was about nine years old, I came home from school to find that Arrow was not in our corral; and in his place was a beautiful, young Palomino horse. My father never said so, but I always suspected that Arrow had died and that this was my father's attempt to replace him.

BD Boy was very different from Arrow. Being a young horse, he was full of energy and could be a real challenge to ride. I found him to be a lot of fun, but had to be on my guard when he decided that he would like to buck. He had an odd sense of humor that would cause him to slow down just to see if you would ask him to speed up. He delighted in testing my riding skills. He would test the security of his bit by pulling his head out, and if the reins slipped through my hands easily, he knew that I didn't have a steady grip. And if my grip wasn't firm, it wasn't long before he selected his moment and would try bucking me off.

The main thing I learned from **BD Boy** was to never give up. He taught me persistence, as well as the need to constantly observe my horse's mood and subtle signs, and to be ready to respond to any action he might take.

Blue

BD Boy was my favorite horse until my father bought a horse for himself named Blue. Blue was a green-broke, four-year-old Grullia horse, from which he got his name. He was a blue buckskin with a black dorsal stripe on his back and stripes along the backs of his legs. Grullia horses were rarely seen in our area, so no matter where I took him he always drew a crowd.

The first summer Blue lived with us, my father made me promise that I wouldn't ride him. Dad was afraid that the horse was too much for me, and that I would get hurt. Well, I made that promise reluctantly, and every afternoon when my father wasn't around, would ride Blue in our corral. I found that despite my father's apprehensions, I was able to control him; and I continued to ride him in the corral until he was gentle enough to take him down by the river.

Everyday that summer I rode Blue to a place called "Rainbow Ranch" owned by a horse trainer named Frosty Straight. Frosty was an old-time cowboy, but he used natural horse training techniques to produce some of the nicest horses in Northern Colorado. Frosty really liked me and worked with me over the summer on training Blue and making sure that he had a solid training foundation. He taught me the importance of groundwork, how to get a horse to give his head to you and bend his body, how to walk straight without crookedness, and how horses should stay supple and not lean on the bit. Frosty stressed "self carriage" in a nice collected frame to promote long-term health. He also stressed the importance of praise and positive reward to get a horse to respond properly to his training.

One evening at the end of the summer, I lost track of time and when I came riding home on Blue, there was my father. At first he was furious that I would lie to him about riding Blue. But when I showed him what I had taught Blue, all he could do was shake his head and say "Well if you have put that much time into him, I suppose you should have him." That was the first time I learned the meaning of the old saying "It is better to seek forgiveness than to ask permission."

From that summer on, Blue placed in almost every horse show in which I entered him. Judging him only from his appearance, you would believe that he was just a horse of average athletic ability. But his great heart and character allowed him to accomplish things beyond his raw athletic ability. From Blue I learned that you can't judge a book by its cover, or a horse by his external appearance.

BUM

In the late 1960's horse showmanship events such as dressage and jumping started to grow in popularity in the Greeley area. To me this seemed to present a whole new direction in which to expand my riding skills and I quickly signed up for jumping lessons.

The horse I had at this time was a big, black, quarter horse cross named "Bum". I soon learned that he was as enthusiastic about jumping as I was. He was the kind of horse you dream about. Bum was a true athlete that loved about any equine sport. I rode him in a cross-section of events, but our favorite sport was polo. While on the CSU polo team, he delighted in checking the other horses and racing to drive the ball to the goal.

Bum was one of those horses that just wanted to please, and would do absolutely anything that I asked of him. He was my companion for 21 years. He helped me through a divorce, kept me sane while I was getting my degrees from college, and loved me everyday of his life. He was the perfect example of how horses have unconditional love for their people. He didn't care if I looked bad, was sad and crying, or was elated about being in love. Bum just loved me. He was a joyful horse and got pleasure from everything we tried. Bum was fast, big, and kind – he taught me unconditional love, joy, and trust.

In these last few pages, I have shared some of the things horses have taught me over the years. I would like you to reflect on the horses in your life and what they have contributed to the person you are today. The only regret I have in my personal assessment of how horses have built my character is that I didn't understand more at the time how I could have contributed to their spirit. At that time, equine therapy wasn't widely promoted in Western cultures and was looked on as a Zen-like, somewhat suspicious, thing to do. Complementary therapy wasn't well understood and only veterinary medicine was practiced.

In my opinion, Arrow's aged body could have greatly benefited from massage because it would have removed metabolic waste buildup and balance the energy in his body. For BD Boy, I think his bucking could well have been caused by a sore back. Massaging him might have relieved his back and hip soreness. Domino was clearly getting revenge for some mistreatment he had in the past. Massage for him could have built a better human/horse relationship and trust. Blue was such a great athlete that his entire body would have benefited from massage. His self-carriage and posture would have improved with regular massage sessions. For Bum, the super horse, massage could have eased the stress of his athletic activities, increased his performance, and might even have provided him with an increased life span.

Through equine massage you will have the ability to make profound changes in the nature and quality of your horse's lives. Whether your horse loves you like Arrow or tolerates you like Domino, it is still possible to develop a good human-horse relationship. Through equine massage, you will have the ability to create better health, performance, and trust with your equine companion.

Chapter 3:

40 Years Later – Equine Therapy

Throughout college, I continued riding Bum and participating in equine sporting events. After college, I joined Hewlett-Packard as a high-tech marketing engineer. This professional career curtailed my riding in shows, but allowed me to change my focus to trail riding. After working for Hewlett-Packard for 25 years, retirement age was approaching, and I was looking for a profession that would allow me to combine my education with my passion for horses. What I found was equine therapy. Equine therapy allowed me to be pro-active in helping horses. It afforded me an opportunity to help them recover from physical or emotional trauma, and to maximize their health, performance and well-being.

Shadow

It was a horse named Shadow that led me to equine therapy. Shadow had been a barrel racing horse that was driven to the point of exhaustion. He had soured out on barrel racing and was troubled enough to hurt you if you forced him to compete any further.

A few years earlier I had lost the equine love of my life, Bum, to a case of colic. For a long time after that I was not able to even be with horses, such was the extent of my grieving. But finally, I came to the realization that horses were too important a part of my life to be without them, and that it was time to bring an equine companion back into my world.

When I first saw Shadow, I knew he was going home with me. It was all in the eye. As I looked into his eye, I could see a very troubled horse that desperately needed a kind, understanding home. He had these big brown eyes that melted you straight into his soul. He had a magnificent black body that was beautiful, but also showed the signs of being overused in competition. His hocks had joint capsule damage from the stress of turning tight little circles at full speed. Looking into his eye, I sensed the worried look that comes from too many years of being forced to run the barrels. To him, barrel racing was a job – a job that he hated.

He had lost faith in people and didn't trust them any longer. I could see that he didn't understand how they could make him continue to hurt himself. This nervousness from being pressed into a competition that he dreaded had taken its toll on his body, and it was evident that he was underweight. But in spite of all of this, I knew that this was the horse for me. It's all in the eye, and his eye had that look that can captivate your soul. At that moment, I knew that he needed me as much as I needed him. When I bargained with the owner to determine his price, I had to stand beside him. If I were to stand where I could look into his eye, I would have paid any price for him.

It took me 18 months to get him over thinking that he had to "run like the wind" when I stepped into the stirrup. Even with all the work I had done with him, Shadow still was not ready to place his trust in me. He had not shaken the worried look and still harbored a deep sense of fear. I knew that if I was going to reach him and bring him out of his worry and fear, I had to find a way to make a deeper connection.

I tried several types of therapy with limited results. Finally, a friend told me about equine massage. I knew that human massage was a popular practice that could yield marvelous benefits, but I had never before thought about massaging a horse and the benefits it might have. Personally, I loved a good massage and could only extrapolate what it might be like for a horse. If you think about it, we only touch horses with devices like brushes, blankets, saddles and bridles. Most of the time we don't really touch our horses. Sure we give them treats and pet their heads, but we don't really feel their muscles.

I decided that if I was going to bring Shadow out of his fearful place and make him an exceptionally good horse, I was going to have to make a deeper connection with him. And I also decided that massage was going to be the means to reach that end. As a result, I enrolled in a local massage school called EquiTouch. From the first horse I touched in these classes, I knew that equine massage was going to be my road to helping as many horses as I could. It was an epiphany that totally changed my life.

As luck would have it, six month's after I graduated from equine massage school, Hewlett-Packard exited the **CD ROM** business and laid off **6,000** of its employees. I was in that first wave of "work force adjustment" (the going euphemism at the time for layoffs) and got a nice compensation package for my years of service. With this money, I set up my own business, called "Horses & Hands", through which I was able to provide equine massage and other services to horse owners.

Through massage, Shadow taught me that even if you are broken, you can learn to be whole again and trust.

Equine Massage as a Business

As I developed my Horses & Hands business, my services included not only performing equine massage, but expanded into conducting clinics for horse owners to teach them how to develop deeper connections with their horses through massage. As my clients wanted to know more about helping their horses, I began giving "Introduction to Equine Massage" clinics for horse owners. I even provided "ranch sitting" services for some clients who had not been on vacation for many years because they had not been able to find anyone they could trust to care for their horses while they were gone. It was during these ranch sitting sessions that I had the opportunity to come into more than casual contact with a wide variety of horses, and to get a chance to see and understand a broader spectrum of equine personalities.

As my equine massage business grew and flourished, I found myself caring for a large number of horses – too large to easily keep track of them all. But as luck would have it my husband, John, who is a physicist by training, currently makes his living doing software development. To help me out, he developed a software program for the personal computer that keeps a record of all the horses I work on, their owners and locations, who their vet is, and other pertinent information. In addition, it allows me to quickly and easily enter the details of an equine massage session and automatically generate a professional-looking report for my clients. This report explains what I found, the strokes I used to address these issues, and other valuable information about the condition of the horse's muscles for their owner.

Since I found this program so useful in my business, I began offering it for sale to other equine massage therapists under the name "EquiTracker™-Massage". To date, we have sold hundreds of copies to massage therapists around the country as well as internationally. It takes a "patchwork" business like mine (massage, clinics, ranch sitting, and selling software and books) to make a living in the Equine Therapy industry. When one segment isn't busy the next segment seems to explode with activity. I am very blessed to have so many clients and horses in my life. Everyday, I get to touch horses and make their lives a little better. It is my greatest desire to extend this reach to as many horse owners as possible, and to impart to them the ability to be a positive force in the better health and well-being of their own horses.

Making the Multi-Level Connection

This book is not intended to make you into a professional massage therapist, but rather to help you make a multi-level connection with your horse through massage. Equine massage has allowed me to make a multi-level connection with Shadow and helped me develop him into a happy, trusting, courageous riding companion. It has been my experience within my equine massage practice, that after the first massage, most of the horses I perform therapy on really crave the deep appreciation and caring that massage provides for their health. Massage is not only a physical connection of kneading muscles, but also a physiological and psychological connection with the horse. It allows you to assess the state of their well-being, both emotionally and physically. Dr. Deb Bennett stated that the really deep solutions to improving a horse's health and well-being starts with the horse's spirit and emotions, not with advanced training and drilling. The bridge to your horse's innermost thoughts and feelings is Love.

To nurture his body and spirit, you must provide the basic essentials of proper nutrition, dental, and ferrier care. Your horse must have adequate turnout with other horses and have available shelter. He must have both work time (a job) so that he feels needed, as well as having turnout to nurture his spirit and emotions. All work and no play makes way for an angry, burned out horse (just like humans). If your tack isn't fitting properly, or you're using severe devices to gain control of your horse, you won't get unhindered natural movement and maximized performance. The more appreciation you give your horse, the harder he will work for you. Your connection will become a true human/horse relationship.

When it comes time to ride, you can increase your success in the saddle by preparing yourself and your horse for the ride. You also need to truly be with your horse by un-cluttering your mind. You need to make sure that your tack fits properly. And you need to prepare your body and that of your horse for maximum movement by stretching.

In the following chapters, I will take you through the detailed steps that you can follow to make each of these requirements happen.

And finally, after a great day of riding, honor your equine companion by treating him to a good massage.

Chapter 4:

Human, Get Your Mind Ready To Ride

Three simple things you can do at home to unclutter your mind, increase balance, stability, whole-body coordination, and body focus.

Before you can be an effective rider, you must release your mind and forget the challenges of your life. If you are preoccupied, your horse will know it. It has been my experience that when I'm not 100% with my horse, that is when accidents are more likely to happen. I miss subtle signs that the horse is giving me that might prepare me for any unexpected movement or reaction. Horses reflect back whatever we are projecting like a mirror into our soul.

The reason I am including the next two chapters is because it is absolutely necessary to have a clear mind and be totally with your horse to successfully perform a quality massage. And the stretches are key to increasing his range of motion and releasing issues that will increase his performance, health, and trust in you.

Left-Brain, Right-Brain Connection

Research has shown that the brain is divided into two hemispheres – the left and the right. The left is responsible for rational thought and language, while the right is responsible for creative thought and visualization. When these two hemispheres are connected, they work together to produce a healthy working brain.

It has been shown that dyslexia is linked with not allowing infants to crawl. As a child, I can remember when women with infants got together, they wanted to be the first to have their baby starting to walk. Fifteen years later, it was those children that were pushed to walk first that had the most trouble with dyslexia.

The left-brain, right-brain connection is a contra-lateral exercise, similar to walking in place. It forces signals to go to both sides of your brain. It accesses both brain hemispheres simultaneously, and is an ideal warm-up for all activities requiring crossing the body's lateral midline. It improves binocular vision, left-to-right eye movement, and improves left/right coordination and balance. These are all essential for good riding balance and stability.

Stand with your feet shoulder width apart. Lift your left arm and hand along with the right knee and leg. Return them to the normal standing position, and immediately lift your right arm and your left knee. Keep alternating these movements as if you are marching in place, and "march on" for a minute or so.

Stabilizing and Grounding

This is a "grounding and balancing" exercise that helps you with whole-body coordination and body focus. It is a lengthening activity that relaxes the hips and sacrum by lengthening the iliopsoas muscle group. It will improve your stability and balance. It also gives you better range-of-motion and flexibility in your hip flexors.

Start with your legs comfortably apart. Point your right foot towards the right. Keep the left foot pointed straight ahead. The heel of the bent leg (right) is aligned with the instep of the straight leg (left). Now bend the right knee as you exhale, and then inhale as you straighten the right leg. The bending knee glides, in a straight line, out over the foot and no further than the arch. Keep your hips tucked under. The torso and pelvis sit squarely, facing the front; the head, bending knee, and foot of the bent leg face to the side. You will feel the stretch on the inside muscles of the straight-leg side. Repeat three times. Now do the left side.

Activate the Brain

This exercise stimulates the carotid arteries that supply freshly oxygenated blood to the brain. It improves body balance, may alleviate visual stress, and gives greater relaxation to the neck and shoulder muscles. An alert mind prepares you for any situation that may come up during your ride.

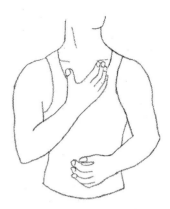

Rub deeply just below the collarbone, to the right and left of the sternum (there are little divots for your fingers to fall into), while holding your other hand over your navel. Stimulate these points for twenty to thirty seconds, or until any tenderness is released. These points may be tender at first; but over a few days to a week the tenderness will subside. After that, simply holding the points will activate them.

Now that you have stimulated energy in the brain and uncluttered your mind so that you can be "totally" with your horse, you are ready to get your body physically prepared to ride.

Chapter 5:

Stretching Exercises for Horse and Rider

*Always check with your health care provider before
starting this or any other exercise routine.*

Basic Rider Stretches – Get Your Body Working

Since riding is an athletic activity, it's important to build strength, balance, and flexibility in order to be a strong rider. By getting fit, you will improve your riding and it will help you prevent accidents and injury. Strengthening your core muscles (abdominals, lower back, hips, butt, and upper legs) will improve your riding posture and help protect your back from possible injury.

Today, there are many programs that can help you build your core strength, but the one I like best and have had the most success with is Pilates training. You can watch your local paper for palates classes, purchase a videotape, or purchase one of the many books published on the subject. You will really be amazed at how much better you ride after building the strength of your core muscles. Mary Midkiff has designed another really great program for building strength, balance, and flexibility. Her book is "Fitness, Performance and the Female Equestrian". This program is designed specifically for women and addresses the difference in anatomy between men and women. You can visit Mary's website at www.womenandhorses.com.

All stretches presented in Equine Muscle Magic can be done in the barn without lying down on the floor. Balance, flexibility, and strengthening are the key to being a physically powerful rider. Stretching increases your flexibility and range-of-motion. Incorporating balance exercises in your routine will help you "stay" in the saddle when your horse makes sudden movements and turns. Strengthening exercises also makes the cues (aids) you give to your horse stronger and clearer.

For stretching to be effective, it must be incorporated into your daily routine. In this chapter, we are taking a whole-body approach by presenting stretches for your arms, shoulders, back, buttock, waist, chest, thighs, hamstrings, and lower leg.

Your muscles should always be warmed prior to any stretching or exercise routines. Warm up for five to ten minutes. You could easily do this by walking your horse around an arena or by going out to the pasture and walking him back to the barn.

For these exercises, do two to three sets of **10-15** repetitions of each. It is not necessary to do all of these exercises every time. From the following exercises, select the ones that best fit your needs.

Chest and Shoulder Stretch

This stretch is perfect for doing in the barn. Find a vertical edge, such as the barn door, cross-tie post, or end of a stall. Stand close to the edge with your arm next to it. Raise your arm to create a 90-degree angle at your elbow, and press your forearm against the vertical edge (post, door jam, etc.) Turn your head and look away from the vertical edge to add a stretch for your neck. Hold the stretch for five seconds. Repeat on both sides.

Benefit: Improves your riding position by opening the chest and stretching your pectoral muscles and shoulders. Helps you sit tall in the saddle and reinforces riding with your shoulders back.

Stretch Tight Hamstrings and Calf Muscles

This stretch can be done using a closed stall door, an arena-rail, or any horizontal surface you can place your hands on. Stand half a body's length from the horizontal surface with your feet shoulder-width apart. Bend at the waist and place your hands on top. Your arms, shoulders and back should be flat. Relax your neck, breath deep, and let your body settle back into the stretch.

Benefit: Helps you have deep heels when riding and promotes good posture for mounting.

Create Flexibility in Your Hamstrings and Calves

Stand with your feet slightly apart, and cross your right leg over the left. Your right leg will be slightly bent and your left leg will be straight. Bend at the hips and reach for the ground. You will feel the stretch in your lower back and calves. If you need added balance, rest your hands on your front leg. Repeat on the other side, crossing your left leg over the right leg.

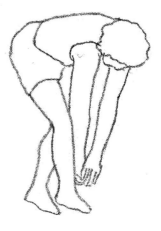

Benefit: Helps stretch your back for riding in a sitting trot, and makes it easier for you to achieve a heels-down riding position.

Stretch Hip Flexors and Develop Balance

With your arms at your side, stand tall and lift your right foot off the ground while bending your right knee. You may want to pick one point in front of you to focus your eyes and help find your balance. Once you can hold this pose, place your right foot against your left leg and rotate at your hip pointing your knee to the side. Rotate your knee to a neutral position, and put your foot down. Repeat with your left leg.

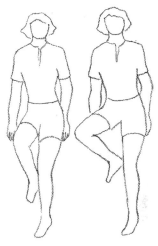

Benefit: Improves your security and balance in the saddle. Reinforces posture and stretches tight hip flexors.

Build Leg Muscles and Strengthen Your Gluteus Muscles (buns)

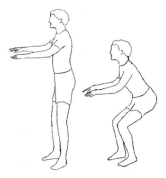

Stand with your feet slightly more than shoulder-width apart. Use your arms for balance in front of you; sit back as if you were sitting down in a chair. Your knees should not go over your toes. From this squatting position, stand back up.

Benefit: Helps you maintain security in the saddle by building strength in your legs and glutes.

Basic Horse Stretches

I have selected five different passive equine stretches that will give your horse maximum range of motion. These should be performed before and after your riding session. Passive stretches are performed by a dismounted person from the ground, while active stretches are done as part of a training program with the rider mounted in the saddle.

As with humans, the horse's muscles should be properly warmed prior to stretching. This can be accomplished by leading your horse at a walk for five to ten minutes. Stretching cold muscles can cause injury. The reason you want to perform the stretches prior to your ride is to help lengthen muscle fibers and give your horse better range-of-motion prior to working. This will help reduce the stress on the muscles and help you keep from straining or creating muscle tears. Be guided by your horse's reactions that reveal his comfort level with the stretches you are performing.

Be aware of your horse's comfort zone. Any sign of discomfort with the stretch should mandate an immediate release of the stretch back to your horse's comfort zone. Signs of discomfort include head tossing, ears set backwards (pinning of ears), resistance in the jaw, or resistance against the stretch. Stretching after a workout helps relax the muscles and releases tightness built up from the workout. In addition, it encourages waste-product removal, improves energy supply, and enhances nerve proprioception.

Muscles, ligaments and tendons in an older horse are less flexible and need more stretching than those of a young horse. Be aware that it will take longer to get an older horse's muscles warmed up, and caution should be used to guard against overstretching. For older horses lateral stretching that makes them move the vertebral column really adds to their flexibility and suppleness. As with so many things in life, less is more. Start out gradually and build up to holding the stretch for 15 seconds. Overstretching can cause painful cramping and increased tension in the muscles. Never hold a stretch for more than 20 seconds.

You must treat each horse as an individual and perform stretches that address his specific needs. Equine muscles start to stretch within five seconds and should be held from 5 to 20 seconds. You should start small and gradually build up to 20 seconds. Always be aware of the horse's comfort zone and reactions to your stretching.

Hip Flexor and Stifle Extension

The first stretch is a Hip Flexor and Stifle Extension. It is good for stretching the gluteus and hamstring muscles.

- Face the rear of the horse and grasp the hind-leg at the fetlock or pastern.

- Lift the toe about 4" off the ground. Remember, we are not doing a

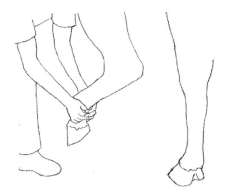

flexion test. Keep the hoof close to the ground to get maximum benefit from this stretch. Lifting the foot too high puts excess pressure on the hock.

- Direct the toe forward, toward the back of the front hoof, keeping the leg in a natural line of movement.

- Let the horse determine how much you pull toward the front hoof. As you do more of this stretch, your horse will gain better range of motion, and you will be able to get the hind toe closer to the back of the front hoof.

- Hold for 15 to 20 seconds. Repeat on the other side.

Shoulder Rotation

The second stretch is a shoulder rotation, which loosens the pectoral muscles, the Serratus Ventralis muscle in the neck (which will help with lateral flexion), and the Intercostal Fascia (which will aid in breathing). It also helps relax the ligaments of the shoulder. In this stretch, your body is acting like a tripod for holding and rotating the shoulder.

- Stand facing horse's forelegs.

- Pick up the leg as though you are going to clean the hoof.

- Face the horse's shoulder, placing both hands over the top of the cannon bone with your fingers facing downward.

- Stand close to the horse to make sure you aren't pulling outward (abduction), keeping the shoulder in line with the horses body.

- Lifting from your knees, gently rotate his shoulder in a clockwise motion (making 2 to 3 rotations).

- Pause for a few seconds and rotate counter clockwise. Repeat on the other side.

Buttock Tuck

The third stretch is a buttock tuck which is good for abdominal strengthening. It stretches the Gluteals, strengthens the back and causes the horse to use it's Rectus Abdominus muscle which is the predominant muscle used for self carriage and collection. Use this stretch to strengthen the horse's back.

- Stand behind the horse.
- Place the palms of your hands over Tuber Ischii (point of butt) on each side of the horse.

- Gently push forward and slightly downward.
- The horse should tuck his butt under, causing his back to round in his loin area (lower back). If not, locate the depression just above the Tuber Ischii in the Semitendinosus (spot where your fingers fall when you have the point of the butt (Tuber Ischii) in the palm of your hand) and scratch vigorously with your fingers and thumbs.

Shoulder Extension

The fourth stretch is a shoulder extension which lengthens the muscles of the shoulder and gives your horse better range of motion for those great front leg extensions. This stretches the Trapezius, Latissimus Dorsi, Serratus Ventralis, Deltoid, and Triceps.

- Stand facing your horse.
- Grasp the leg just above the fetlock joint and pick up the leg.
- Place one hand on the back of the cannon bone and the other behind the knee.

- Gently and slowly pull the horse's knee toward your knee.
- Hold for 5 to 10 seconds. Repeat on the other side.

Lateral Neck Stretch

The fifth stretch is a lateral neck stretch, which will help improve the horse's neck flexibility.

- While your horse's head is facing forward, allow him to sniff an incentive such as a cookie, a carrot, etc.

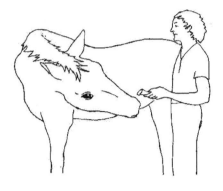

- Then gently guide his head back by pulling the incentive toward his withers.

- Maximum stretch result is obtained by keeping the horse's head horizontal to the ground.

- The horse will release this stretch when the incentive is eaten (5 to 10 seconds). Repeat on the other side.

A Benefit to Horse and Rider

Taking the time to do these stretches will reward the rider with more strength and better posture in the saddle, and help prevent the horse from straining or injuring his muscles, giving both horse and rider a better ride.

In the next chapter, we will explore how improper equipment fit can lead to poor performance and behavioral problems.

Chapter 6:

Subtle Signs of Soreness, and Tack Fit

The Importance of Tack Fit

Proper tack fit cannot be overemphasized. Horses bodies change over time, which means you must check often how the horse's tack is fitting him. A qualified saddle-fitter should be consulted prior to purchasing a saddle. When I was growing up, we fit the saddle to the rider and didn't give much thought about the horse. One saddle was used to ride all the horses, regardless of size. We just kept adding saddle blankets or taking them away until we had the saddle comfortably built-up above the withers. We didn't give much thought to how the saddle might be pinching or rubbing the horse, as long as it fit the rider. Thank God those days are over and we have electronic saddle fitting and master saddle-fitters to consult.

We now have technology that can help us see where the saddle is pinching, rubbing, or bridging. Yes it is an additional cost, but well worth the investment to have your saddle custom fitted. Once the saddle fits the horse properly, his mind will be on what you are trying to teach him rather than where it hurts. If you, as the rider, are having trouble staying balanced in the saddle, that is a primary indicator that your saddle probably isn't fitting the horse's back properly.

All tack should be checked if your horse has gained or lost weight. Additionally, as horses age their backs reflect the signs of gravity. A horse that is getting a lower back needs tack that isn't bridging on his back.

Finally, a word about bridle fit. If your horse is yawning after you remove the bridle, this can be a sign that the brow-band is too tight. Additionally, if there are little sores on the side of his mouth, check for proper bit length and fit.

In a how-to article on the website "thehorse.com", Justine Gandolfo observes that "a poorly fitting bit can cause a myriad of issues including head tossing, getting behind the bit, taking off, and many other problems", and that these are evidence of a generally unhappy horse. For more information on how to determine if your horse's tack fits well, go to Sharon Biggs' online article at "HorseChannel.com".

Subtle Signs of Soreness

The only way horses can show us that something is wrong is through attitude. All too often I have heard horse owners say that their horse is just being a "puke" and not wanting to perform. In reality, the horse is trying to tell them something the only way they know how, through attitude. Typically, the horse is uncomfortable or hurting somewhere. It is our job to discover what is bothering the horse and help him get back to health. We have to be detectives and take a whole-body approach to finding what is wrong.

Watch your horse's movement at rest (in the stall or barn) and at play with other horses. Is he moving freely and playing normally with the other horses? Does he stand square or is he pointing a foot or resting one leg more than the others? Next, watch your horse move from the front, back (standing behind him), and side views. Is his movement fluid and symmetrical? Does he have more muscle build-up on one side? If the muscles are not symmetrical, it could be a sign of not loading his legs evenly; or it may be that the rider is working the horse in one direction more than the other.

Is he flexing his joints evenly on both sides? Is he stumbling or dragging his toes? When you observe him from behind watching him walk away, do his rump muscles rise and fall equally from left to right? If you see the muscle hike up more on one side than the other, it's the hiked side that may be hurting. Watching a horse trot in a circle is one of the easiest ways to see any type of lameness. Watch your horse walk and trot in circles, in both directions, first untacked and then with the saddle on. Are his strides even and are his hoof prints showing even landing?

These are some of the questions you should be thinking about when trying to discover if your horse has soreness in his body. Nothing replaces your veterinarian for determining soreness or lameness; but this will help you recognize potential problems and provide valuable information to your vet.

When horses are not performing up to their previous level of performance, watch for one or more of the following signs:

- Ringing or swishing of the tail
- Pinning the ears
- Shaking the head
- Refusing or resisting leads
- Nostril clinching
- Resisting stretching (if muscles have been warmed)
- Girthing problems – pinning ears, concern with cinching, nipping
- Stride is short or out of balance – improper tracking
- Reluctance to back up (dismounted)
- Sore back or cold back
- Lateral movement difficulties
- Head and neck stiffness (discomfort)
- Hind leg scuffing
- Stumbling
- Change in attitude
- Change in breathing pattern
- Change in muscle tension

It is our job to start eliminating possible causes for these actions. What could account for a change in behavior? Have they had proper dental care? Could your horse's mouth be hurting from points on the teeth? Have you been following a good worming program? Could your horse have a stomach full of parasites? Are you providing proper farrier practices? Is your horse stumbling because he needs his feet trimmed (or new shoes)? When was the last time you had your saddle fitted?

Horses change shape as they age, and gain or lose weight. Nothing is more destructive than a saddle that is too small and pinching. Is his back sore, or does he need a chiropractic adjustment or a massage to work out the tenderness in the muscles? Are his hocks or other joints sore from the activity you have him riding in? Is burnout a possibility? Have you been drilling the horse for certain activities (i.e., loping circles, pivots, fast stops, riding in a collected frame too long, etc.)?

Any of these can be a mystery that needs to be unraveled so your horse can get back to being the perfect horse for you. Horses don't want to be bad, in reality they just want to please.

If you determine that his behavior is caused by sore muscles and not due to soreness in his joints or feet, the massage protocols described in the following chapters can help bring your horse back to maximized performance and health.

Chapter 7:
Equine Massage for
Performance & Health

Musculosketal problems are the most common cause of poor performance. — Tufts University of Veterinary Medicine

Benefits of Massage

Massage can have a number of beneficial effects on your horse. Among these are:

- Massage counteracts toxin buildup, muscle soreness, fluid buildup in the lower limbs, and reduces stress.

- Massage increases circulation and supplies essential nutrients to muscles and aids lymphatic flow.

- Massage is stimulating and relaxing.

- Massage improves flexibility and range-of-motion.

- Massage can reduce the possibility of injury and helps to speed recovery time from injuries.

- Massage maintains muscle health by releasing problem areas.

- Massage lengthens muscle fibers.

- Massage improves the balance and posture of your horse.

- Massage promotes a healthy coat.

- Massage helps to connect you physically, emotionally and psychologically with your horse.

Before you can start massaging, you need to know the "contraindications" for massage. These are situations where doing a massage can cause more harm than good. Always err on the conservative side. If you have any doubts at all, *Don't Massage!*

Massage is contraindicated whenever you observe:

- Inflammation: heat, swelling, pain and redness (you can see some redness in gray and white horses, although this indicator is not very useful in dark-skinned horses)

- Infections or rashes (i.e., hives, fungal or bacterial infections, etc.)

- Skin lacerations or open wounds

- Elevated body temperature

- Dehydration

- Signs of bruising

- Vascular or heart problems (heart problems need to be determined prior to massage)

- Cancer

- Areas of soft tissue calcification

- Pregnancy (you can do *gentle* massage for about the first four months)

- Aftermath of an accident

- Persistent undiagnosed pain

- Cases of colic

- Cases of "tying up" (tying up is a protein imbalance which causes the muscles to contract)

Once you have determined that none of the above contraindications apply, you can prepare yourself for performing the massage. Some of the things you will want to do are preparing your hands for the massage, performing certain exercises to increase your own sensitivity, and learning some techniques for gauging how much pressure to apply as well as which areas of the horse to avoid applying force to.

Getting Your Hands Ready For Massage

*A tactile comparison to everyday items,
and hand exercises.*

Muscle tissue can be relaxed, tight, in spasm, or in any number of states in between. For instance, a muscle can feel soft, warm, and pliable like a piece of wool; this is what a relaxed muscle feels like. Or the muscle can feel very tight and firm like the feel of an apple; this is a muscle in tension. If the muscle feels hard, firm and cold like a leather saddle flap, it is a muscle in spasm.

On the other hand, if you are feeling something that feels like the edge of a cup (hard and rigid), that would be a superficial bone ridge you are feeling. Never massage over a bony structure. Happy muscle feels warm, smooth, and pliable. Unhappy muscle feels cold, dense, stringy and tight.

Your hands have to learn to detect all the different muscle variations to be effective. Developing hand-sensitivity is paramount to performing a good massage. The following three exercises will help develop your sense of feel.

Exercise 1: "The Princess and the Pea"

Take a mane or tail hair from your companion (don't pull it out, just get the ones that end up in your brush) and place it under a sheet of phonebook paper. Then feel for it, if you find it, then increase the number of sheets of paper to two and feel for it again. Keep increasing the paper one sheet at a time until you can't feel the hair under it. There is no right answer about how many sheets you should be able to feel the hair under – you just feel what you feel. With practice the number of sheets will increase as your hand sensitivity increases and as you start trusting what you are feeling.

Exercise 2: Subtle Texture Variations

Take three eggs (you may want to hard boil them if there is a chance you will drop them.) One at a time, close your eyes and feel the surface of each egg for differences. No two eggs are alike and you should begin to feel differences in the way they are formed and subtle differences in their texture. Then describe to yourself how the three surfaces differ. Alternatively, you can do this exercise with three oranges. The purpose of this exercise is to develop a fine sense of subtle differences that will enable you to detect these differences in muscle variations. It is not enough to simply observe these differences, but you must learn to describe the variations in order to direct your focus and thereby increase your sensitivity to them.

Exercise 3: Cornstarch (It's messy, but it's fun!!!)

Dissolve ½ cup cornstarch in about ¼ cup of water. The correct proportion of cornstarch and water is critical. If you have too much cornstarch, it will become dry and flaky and you should add more water. If you have too much water, the mixture will be insufficiently viscous and will act like ordinary liquid. Either add more cornstarch or just play with it for a while until some of the water has evaporated.

If you move your fingers (or the palm of your hand) through it slowly, it acts like a liquid. Warmed equine muscles do the same thing; they just open up and let you spread the muscle fibers.

If you move your fingers (or the palm of your hand) quickly across the top of it, it will act like a solid. Your fingers skip across the top surface of the puddle, leaving it apparently undisturbed. If you move too quickly when massaging muscle, it will stay hard and not allow you to work with the muscle fibers.

In order for the massage strokes to be effective, you need to slow down and sink into the muscles. The purpose of this exercise is to train your hands to move at the correct speed, neither too slow nor too fast, allowing the muscle fibers to open up and release.

After you have increased the sensitivity in your hands to observe the muscle quality and have learned the proper speed to apply pressure, you need to learn how much pressure is appropriate for various areas of the horse and conditions that you will encounter. We will begin this by learning to gauge how much pressure you are actually applying.

Learning to Gauge Pressure

How much pressure should you use? The answer depends on what issue you are trying to get to release. Practice will guide you; and the more you massage, the more your hands will know.

Take a weight scale, like your bathroom scale, and practice evaluating what different pounds of pressure feel like. Try 5 or 10 pounds, then 15 or 20 pounds, and up to 35 pounds. Now try using one finger, then two fingers, and then the whole palm of your hand. Then try the same exercise, applying your body weight. I'm often asked, "Doesn't it take a lot of force to massage horses?" The answer is No. As you can see, it's amazing how easily the weight/force compounds. A finger-stroking touch rates about 0.1 to 1 pound. A light touch is about 2 to 3 pounds. A regular touch is about 3 to 5 pounds. A firm touch is about 8 to 10 pounds. Heaver-muscled horses will take a little more pressure to achieve a firm touch. A heavy pressure starts at 15 pounds. Never use more than about 20 to 25 pounds of pressure; more than that will bruise the muscle fibers.

For a good massage, you can apply pressure that will produce deep bodily effects without causing discomfort. Always begin with light pressure and slowly progress to heavier pressure. Never jab your fingers into the horse; instead, apply firm pressure with the soft pads of the palm of your hand, the fingers, and the thumbs. Visualize using these fleshy pads to rest your body weight. Use your body weight on the pads of your hands, rather than arm strength to apply the pressure. If you force the pressure with the strength of your arm alone, you will be met with resistance.

It is important to stay away from bone ridges, because you can bruise the muscle and hurt the horse. You can recall how it hurts when you hit your elbow on something; that's how it feels to the horse if you rap or apply pressure over any of his bony protuberances. Since these areas are only covered by skin and hair, they are very sensitive.

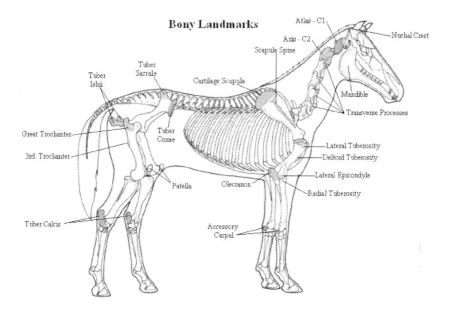

Bony Landmarks

Atlas - C1
Nuchal Crest
Axis - C2
Scapula Spine
Tuber Sacrale
Cartilage Scapula
Tuber Ishii
Mandible
Transverse Processes
Great Trochanter
Tuber Coxae
Lateral Tuberosity
3rd. Trochanter
Deltoid Tuberosity
Lateral Epicondyle
Patella
Olecranon
Radial Tuberosity
Tuber Calcis
Accessory Carpal

To help you identify areas that should not be massaged, I have included a chart called "Bony Landmarks". (A larger version appears in Appendix E) You should learn to identify the location of each of these areas, and avoid knocking on or applying pressure to them.

- The Poll (nuchal crest) is the triangular shape at the very top of the head, where the head comes to a point between the ears.

- The Atlas (the first cervical vertebrae), which can be felt as a semicircle just behind the ears on the neck. The muscle on top of the Atlas can be massaged, but the bony semicircle should not be.

- The Scapular Spine. To find this, run your hand horizontally across the shoulder 4-6 inches below the withers until you feel a raised ridge of bone that is hard like the edge of a cup.

- The Point of the Shoulder (Lateral Tuberosity). To find this, progress vertically down from the Scapular Spine toward the chest until you feel another bony ridge.

- The Elbow (Olecranon) is the chevron-shaped bone just in front of the girth or cinch area.

- The Croup (Tuber Sacrale) is the highest point of the back bone just behind the saddle.

- The Point of the Hip (Tuber Coxae) is found just behind and above the flank.

- The Point of the Butt (Tuber Ishii) is the only bony point you will find on the back of the horse's butt.

- The Stifle Joint (Patella) is at the top of the hind legs.

- The Hock (Tuber Calcis).

In general, all points on the lower leg of the horse should be avoided since it is mostly composed of tendons and ligaments, and there are no muscles in this area that should be massaged except by a professional massage therapist.

Now that you have seen the areas of the horse to avoid, we will next locate and discuss the various muscles that you will be massaging.

The muscles of the horse are divided into several layers, but it is only the superficial muscles (the ones you can feel from the surface) that we will be dealing with here. The deeper layers are not easily accessible.

Of these superficial muscles, the ones located in the neck are perhaps the most important since they control the horse's neck flexion and extension, and lateral movement of the head and neck. Also, the neck can be one of the most difficult areas to massage. This is because it contains 24 pairs of muscles, and some of them can be difficult to locate

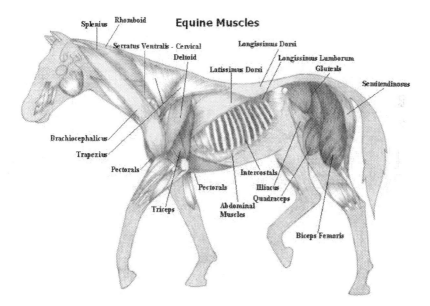

As we discuss these muscles, refer to the muscle diagram above. (A larger version of this diagram can be found in Appendix A)

The following are the main muscles of the neck that you will be massaging. As we go through the muscles below, remember that each muscle is part of a pair and is found on both the left and the right side.

- The Splenius muscles (one on each side) are responsible for extending and elevating the neck when contracted on both sides. When contracted on one side, they are responsible for lateral flexion of the head and neck to that side.

- The Rhomboid muscle has both a cervical and a thoracic portion, which draw the scapula up and forward, as well as up and backward.

- The Trapezius is one of the easiest muscles to find since it is the very visible muscle that forms the "V" shape above the shoulder. It performs the same function as the Rhomboid, but on a more superficial level.

- The Brachiocephalicus is the primary protractor of the foreleg and gives the horse the great extension we are all looking for.

From here we move on to the muscles of the shoulder.

- The Infraspinatus and Supraspinatus muscles act as a lateral ligament of the shoulder and surround the scapular spine. They aid in the movement of the shoulder.

- The Deltoid is responsible for flexing the shoulder and moving the forearm.

- The Latissimus Dorsi is the primary retractor of the front leg. It is the muscle that complements the movement of the Brachiocephalicus; and together they provide the fluid movement of the forelimbs.

- The Triceps muscle is the large, ball-shaped muscle at the base of the shoulder in front and above the elbow. It is responsible for extending the elbow and flexing the shoulder.

- The Pectoral muscles are located on the chest and the girthing area. They help advance the forelimbs and pull them in toward the body.

From here we move on to the muscles of the back and trunk.

- The Longissimus Dorsi (a segmented muscle consisting of cervical, thoracic and lumbar portions), is the longest muscle in the horse's body and extends the back and hollows it out. This is one of the most important muscles to massage since the Lumborium portion sits right behind the saddle, and can be the cause of most back issues with the horse.

- The Intercostal muscles, located between the ribs, aid in breathing. They either pull the ribs forward (to facilitate inspiration/

inhaling) or they pull the ribs backward (to facilitate expiration/exhaling).

- The Abdominal muscles aid in flexing the back to give us a rounded back, and the collected frame we like to ride. The Ring of Muscles chart (Appendix B) lists the muscles and bones responsible for collection.

Finally, we have the muscles of the pelvic limb.

- The Gluteal muscles flex and extend the hip.

- The Hamstrings are made up of the Biceps Femoris, the Semitendinosus, and the Semimembranosus. They are the "power muscles" of the hindquarters.

- The Quadriceps, which surround the Femur, are indicators of the health of the Stifle.

Don't worry if you can't remember the names of all these muscles. I only cover them here to let you know what each of them are responsible for, and so that later when we describe the actual massage techniques, you can refer back to this diagram and locate these muscles. If you want to know more about the functions of these muscles, there are several good veterinary manuals that go into more detail. And in case you are interested, I have included a muscle pronunciation table in Appendix C.

Also included in Appendix F is a diagram of the horse showing the more common names for the various parts of the horse. These will sometimes be used instead of the more technical names when describing which part of the horse we are working on.

Visualization Exercise:

Place yourself inside the body of a horse.

Now that you have seen the muscle structure of the horse from an outside perspective, I have an exercise in which you project yourself inside the horse's body. This will help you get a deeper understanding of how the horse feels, and allow you to empathize with the discomforts the horse might be experiencing.

To begin this exercise, close your eyes and feel what it's like having four legs. How does it feel to walk, trot, and canter? Do you like having your hooves cleaned. How does it feel to have shoes on? Are they heavy? Does it improve or impair your balance? Is there any soreness in your hooves or legs? Since these four legs support your back, how does it feel to have a saddle placed on your back? Is there any soreness in the withers or the loin area? How is your balance affected by the weight of a rider?

Since you are a pray animal, hearing and seeing are vital to your survival. What do you experience seeing through a horse's eyes? What does it sound like to hear through a horse's ears? How does it feel to be covered in hair? Do you like to be brushed fast or slow?

Now, put all these sensations together. I use this exercise to get in touch with the differences between being in the body of a human and being in the body of a horse. I like to do this exercise several times a year to help keep me connected with the feeling of being a horse.

Additionally, when I am working on a horse that has had an accident, like falling down, being run into by another horse, hitting his head on something, etc., I visualize the muscle damage from the accident and the surrounding muscles that will be impaired. For example, if your horse has hurt his shoulder by running into a fence, not only will the muscles of the shoulder need massaging, but his leg, the lower neck in front of the shoulder, the brisket (pectorals), and the withers and shoulder area on that side will need special attention. It's amazing how the "ripple effect" radiates through the accident site and the surrounding muscles. To help eliminate the potential soreness, you should work all muscles connected to the accident site.

Make sure that you are being aware of contraindications for massage. (See Chapter 7) Depending on the severity of the accident, nothing replaces the professional opinion and diagnosis of a qualified veterinarian.

Now that you are aware of the muscles that might require massage, it is time to look at the various massage strokes that you will be using to relieve the stresses in those muscles. This is the subject of the next chapter.

Chapter 8:

Learning the Massage Strokes

There are many different massage strokes that professional equine massage therapists use to address a variety of different muscle conditions and to produce positive results. Some of these, however, if not performed correctly or applied with too much pressure can result in bruising or even harming the horse. For this reason, we will concentrate in this book on four massage strokes that are safer to use, and that will address most of the muscle issues that you will encounter.

These four massage strokes will allow you to open up muscles, alleviate muscle spasms, loosen fascia and knotted tissue, increase lymph circulation, breakdown adhesions, release dense/congested muscle tissue, increase muscle mobility, and improve blood flow. These four simple massage strokes are sufficient to complete any of the massage routines in this text.

- *Effleurage* is a long, smooth continuous stroke, similar to lightly stroking the muscle. It is used to locate any problem areas, assess the state and quality of the muscle tissue, and to build a body map used for planning the massage. Very light pressure should be used. Effleurage promotes relaxation by stimulating a natural opiate release, thus reducing any sensation of pain. Increasing the pressure in your effleurage stroke will act to release fascia adhesions.

- *Compression* strokes are used to alleviate muscle spasms. Compression is a rhythmic pumping action employing the palm and heal of the hand over a specific muscle area. It is administered in an inward and upward manner, using a slight twist of the forearm.

- *Petrissage* is a firm kneading and squeezing of the muscles using circular thumbs, circular fingers, folding and vibration. Petrissage is used to open and release muscles, improve circulation, and loosen fascia and knotted tissue. Fascia is that silvery, white connective tissue that binds the skin to the muscle. For example, if you pull the skin from a chicken breast, fascia is that thin silvery, see-through tissue that connects the skin to the muscle. Fascia is the matrix

of connective tissue that runs top-to-bottom and front-to-back, and surrounds all muscles and bones.

- *Friction* strokes will reduce muscle spasms and release dense or congested muscle tissue, thus producing heat, stripping toxins from tissue and increasing lymph circulation. Friction strokes are done by using the heal of the hand or the tips of the thumbs or fingers across the grain of the muscle to restore tissue mobility and break down any adhesions in the muscle tissue.

You can use any combination of strokes given here. Each stroke has many derivations and you can combine them to fit your own personal massage technique.

The Massage Dance

Massage is a Dance
– a dance between you and your horse.

Please remember that massage is not a way to force your will on your horse. It is a tool to help remove obstacles in his body so that he can work more efficiently, improve his performance, and make that important multi-level connection. Your intention is a vital key in massaging and healing his muscles. Since horses are prey animals, they are tuned to read subtle signals. They are aware of your mood and body language; so breath deep, center yourself, and bring love into your thoughts.

It is important to keep your own body mechanics healthy so that you can massage your horse for years to come. Body alignment is key; bend your knees, bend your hips, straighten your back, and open you chest. This will communicate a relaxed, calm feeling and emotion to the horse.

Body language is so important to achieving a great massage. Center yourself and forget about the challenges of the day. If you are thinking about your shopping list, or what needs to be done at home or in the office, your horse will sense that you are not connected to him.

Centering yourself is simple. You may choose to use exercises from chapter 4. The left brain right brain connection or the stabilizing and grounding exercise are two that work nicely for me. Or you may choose to simply take a few moments and pay attention to your breathing, allowing yourself to relax as you inhale and exhale.

Once you are centered, you may begin thinking about performing your massages. Remember, the massage is totally for the health and well-being of your horse. If during the massage, you become or feel un-centered again, keep one hand on the horse, step back, and pay attention to your breathing until you are again centered.

Always use your fingers as sensors to get feedback on muscle tone and condition. Your fingers should become an extension of your brain, giving you information for adjusting your massage.

If the massage you are doing doesn't feel good to you, it won't feel good to your horse. If you see signs and reactions from the horse like ear pinning, swishing the tail, or moving away from you, you probably are using too much pressure. Also, watch for the good signs, like lowering the head, licking and chewing, sighing, soft eyes, etc. It's these good signs that massage therapists live for! These are the indications that the horse is releasing the issues in his body.

You need to vary the speed and pressure of the massage. A monotone massage is boring for the horse. Remember, the deeper you go, the slower you need to go. You should only open up the muscle fibers as fast as they want to open. *Don't rush!*

Remember to never use direct pressure or knocking on any of the "Bony Landmarks" described in the previous chapter. Additionally, since there aren't any muscles below the knee or hock, only tendons and ligaments, the lower legs should never be included in the massage.

Practice good horse safety. When massaging, always keep a hand on the horse. This contact brings continuity to the massage and keeps you from surprising him. Don't ever let the horse pin you between him and a solid structure such as a stall wall, fence, side of a barn, etc. Always let the horse know where you are. Watch for any reactions or signs from the horse. When working on the hindquarters, keep at least one hand in contact with the horse so that you can push him away if necessary.

Gently and quietly approach your horse, allowing him time to understand what you are trying to achieve – mutual respect and trust.

I start each massage by asking permission (mentally) from my higher power to be used for the "highest and best purpose" of the horse. I also mentally ask the horse for permission to touch his body. You know that permission is given when the horse relaxes, sighs, or gives you a soft eye. Place your hands flat against the horse by his withers area, and then do this mental meditation. It will only take a few moments of calm breathing with the horse to receive permission.

> *"Your hand has the power to hurt me or to heal me.*
> *Look into my eyes, to the heart of my soul*
> *and choose to heal me."*
>
> **– Margritte Coats**

Chapter 9:
A 10-minute Massage

*Three Things You Can Do
To Maintain Your Horse's Performance.*

This is a 10-minute massage that should be done after every ride, or when you don't have time to do a full-body massage. Be sure to let the horse's muscles rest for a few minutes after the ride before starting a massage.

This massage consists of three parts and is done in a cookbook style. These three parts are a shoulder massage, a back massage, and a hindquarters massage with step-by-step directions for each. It is a "one size fits all" protocol that is applied the same way without regard to any specific issues the horse may have.

Since the horse carries 60 percent of its body weight on it's front-end, the shoulders are a key area for muscle fatigue and tension, and are the first area that we will concentrate on.

I selected a back massage for the second part, because the circulation in the horse's back has been restricted by the saddle during a ride. Think about when you wear a pair of tight-fitting pants. When you take them off, the waistband area itches because the blood flow (circulation) has been restricted by the

69

waistband.   In a similar way, blood-flow restriction occurs in the horse from the saddle and pad.

The third part of the 10-minute massage is the hindquarter massage, which is important for removing any metabolic waste build-up in the muscles and promoting better range-of-motion. The hindquarters act like the power train in a car, providing all the forward propulsion and speed.

Shoulder Massage – Increase the range-of-motion in the shoulder and front leg extension.

Start by standing on the left side of your horse, by his shoulder, facing toward his rear end. Begin with an Effleurage stroke which is a long smooth stroke coming up the shoulder, circling around the scapula, and coming down to the point of the shoulder. Repeat this three times, each time adding just a little more pressure. Make sure that you are not on top of the Scapular Spine which runs vertically down the shoulder. If you are on the spine it will feel hard like the ridge of a coffee cup.

1 Shoulder Massage

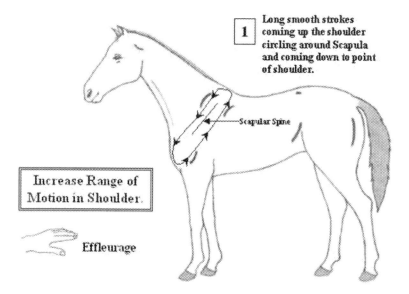

1 Long smooth strokes coming up the shoulder circling around Scapula and coming down to point of shoulder.

Scapular Spine

Increase Range of Motion in Shoulder.

Effleurage

Next use a Compression stroke. Make smooth half circle strokes on the Triceps muscle, moving toward the elbow. Use the heal of your hand administered in an inward and upward manner. Repeat three times. This action reduces stress in the shoulder and elbow.

 # 2 Triceps Massage

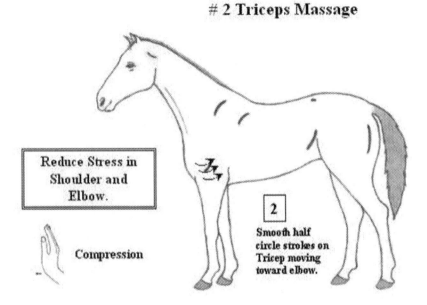

Reduce Stress in
Shoulder and
Elbow.

Compression

2

Smooth half
circle strokes on
Tricep moving
toward elbow.

Now switch directions and face toward the head of the horse while still standing by his left shoulder. You are going to work on the muscles of his upper leg using a Petrissage stroke. Take your left hand and cup the muscles of his upper leg, pushing the muscles forward and around to the inside of the leg. Let your hand slip around the leg like you are kneading bread. Repeat three times. This action helps to increase front-leg extension.

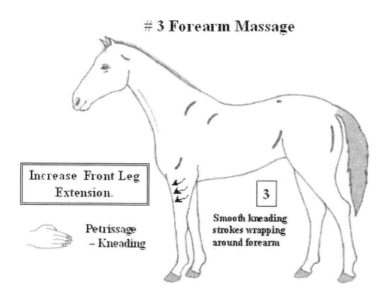

3 Forearm Massage

Increase Front Leg Extension.

Petrissage - Kneading

3

Smooth kneading strokes wrapping around forearm

Back Massage – Increase Circulation and Reduce Back Stress

Stand facing the horse just behind the withers. Place the fingers of your left hand on the horse's back at the top of the spine. Make sure not to use any pressure on the spine itself. We are using the spine only as a guide to help you down the back. Use a Compression stroke in a smooth pumping action with the heal of the hand moving horizontally along the back toward the hip. It's like you are drawing a series of little half-circles up the back. Repeat three times.

4 Back massage

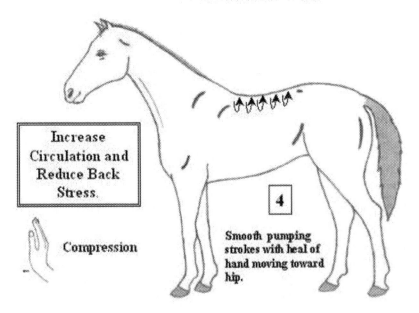

Increase Circulation and Reduce Back Stress.

Compression

4

Smooth pumping strokes with heal of hand moving toward hip.

Hindquarter massage – Part A – Increase Range-Of-Motion and Hind Leg Movement

Stand back to the left of the horse's tail, facing forward toward the head of the horse. Using an Effleurage stroke, you will make long smooth strokes with the flat of the hand, starting at the top of the butt muscle and moving toward the flank. Repeat three times.

#5 Hindquarter Massage

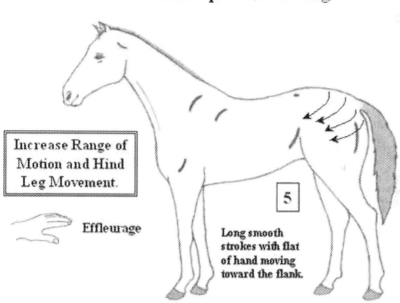

Increase Range of Motion and Hind Leg Movement.

Effleurage

5

Long smooth strokes with flat of hand moving toward the flank.

While still standing back by the horses tail, facing forward, you are going to work on his gaskin (upper-leg) muscles. Using a Petrissage stroke, just like you used on the front legs, take your left hand and cup the muscles of his upper leg. Push the muscles forward and around to the inside of the leg. Let your hand slip around the leg like you are kneading bread. Repeat three times.

#6 Hindquarter Massage - Gaskin

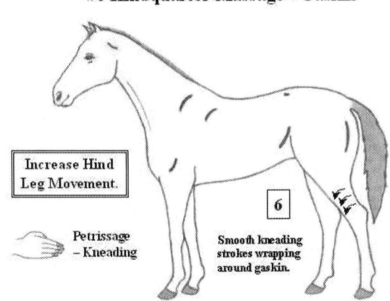

Increase Hind Leg Movement.

Petrissage – Kneading

6

Smooth kneading strokes wrapping around gaskin.

Hindquarter massage – Part B – Increase Propulsion and Ability to Run

This is where you use a Friction stroke across the muscle fibers of the hamstrings. Stand to the left side of the tail facing toward the head. Using your right hand, place your fingers along the butt area next to the tail, and draw them out to the side. Use smooth half circle strokes on the Hamstrings, moving away from the tail. Repeat three times.

#7 Hindquarter Massage - Hamstrings

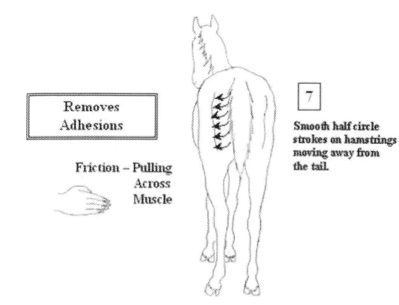

Removes
Adhesions

Friction – Pulling
Across
Muscle

7

Smooth half circle
strokes on hamstrings
moving away from
the tail.

The last step is to place your hands on the top of the croup and do long smooth strokes coming down the hindquarters, moving toward the hocks. Visualize the muscle fibers smoothing out as you are completing this stroke. Repeat three times.

#8 Hindquarter Massage – Smoothing Hamstrings

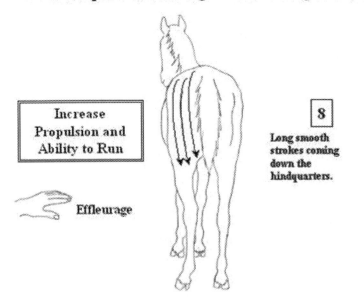

Increase Propulsion and Ability to Run

Effleurage

8

Long smooth strokes coming down the hindquarters.

When you have finished with the left side of the horse, move to the right side and perform these same sets of massages. Start with the shoulder massage and continue through the upper-leg, back, and hindquarters massages. You may have to switch hands to effectively massage the right side of the horse.

The following illustration is a summary of the strokes used in the "10-Minute Massage to Better Performance and Health". I designed this to be copied and hung up in the barn for reference. Many of my clients laminate it to protect it from dust and spills.

Summary – 10 Minute Massage

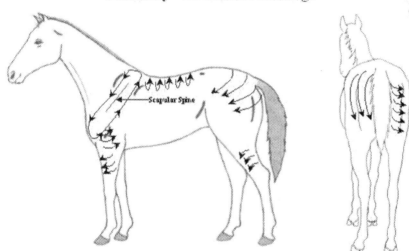

79

Chapter 10:

Building the "Body Map"

*You build a Body Map to provide a guide
for the full-body massage.*

Before I start any massage, I first build a "body map" of the horse. This is a mental picture of all the horse's muscles and any issues I find with them. This is the beginning of a free-form massage where you treat each horse as an "individual" and massage his body based on the issues you find while building this body map. It is key to performing an effective massage.

Of the strokes we discussed earlier, an Effleurage stroke is used to build the body map. It is a very light stroke designed to give you information, coming through your hands, about the tone and quality of the horse's muscles. If you are having trouble feeling, instead of using your whole hand, roll up onto your fingertips and use only the pads of the fingers to give you data. Additionally, make sure that you aren't using too much pressure; it is easier to feel the tone and quality of the muscle with a light touch. In building a body map "less pressure is more". If you are using too much pressure it may overwhelm the information you are receiving.

Effleurage should be done very quickly. It should only take you 5 to 7 minutes to do Effleurage on the whole horse (that's 2 ½ to 3 ½ minutes per side). If you are taking more time than that, you are over thinking the information and causing the building of the body map to be more difficult than it needs to be.

Building the body map is the only time that I do one entire side of the body and then go to the other side and do the same thing. You need single sided continuity to build the body map.

To build the body map, I start my stroke at the poll and work down the neck with long-smooth strokes, working my way back to the butt. I do the front legs, then the shoulder and barrel, and end by going over the butt and down the hind leg. I then step to the other side of the horse start at the poll again and work back to that side's hindquarters. Once you have identified the major problem areas, and have built your body map, it is time to begin the massage. Be sure to mentally ask the horse for permission to massage.

The following paragraphs will cover each of these areas in detail, showing you how to develop the body map information.

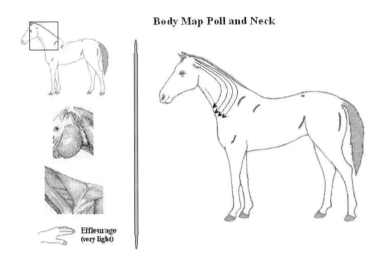

Body Map Poll and Neck

Effleurage
(very light)

I start at the poll, feeling for tension buildup in the horse's Atlas area. Then I progress with long, smooth strokes along the top of the neck toward the shoulder. At the shoulder, I curve down the ridge in front of the shoulder to the point of the shoulder. Along this ridge I'm feeling for tightness and knots. Knots won't feel hard like a "pea", but rather more like a shapeless area of dense, tight muscle.

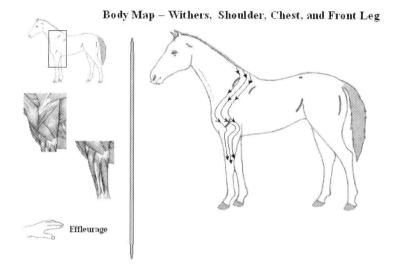

Body Map – Withers, Shoulder, Chest, and Front Leg

Effleurage

Next I feel the shoulder area. I start at the withers feeling for congestion and tension above the Scapula. I then quickly move to the entire shoulder blade. I glide my fingers down both sides of the Scapular Spine to the point of the shoulder. I then go to the Triceps muscle and feel the muscle all the way to the elbow. At this point I feel the Pectoral muscles (chest) both in front of the leg and over the girth area. Then I progress down the left-front leg, stopping at the knee. I will feel below the knee to make sure that the lower leg isn't too hot or too cold, and progress to the pastern above the hoof feeling for puffiness or heat. Heat or cold in these areas will not affect how the massage will be performed, but is information that the owner should be made aware of.

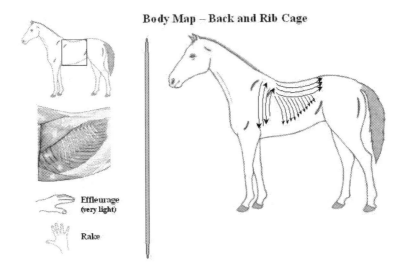

Body Map – Back and Rib Cage

Effleurage
(very light)

Rake

From here I begin feeling the muscle tone and quality of the back. I pay particular attention to the area just behind the withers which can have issues resulting from poor saddle fit. Then I progress down the muscles just behind the shoulder to the girth area. These muscles can be hard and feel like baseballs in horses that pull from their front legs rather than driving from their rear legs. Horses worked in a collected frame will have fit muscles in this area, but not over-built muscles. I then start tracing lines, using the vertebral column as a guide for finding tension in the back. I will move from the withers to the lower-back area (also called loin), checking for tightness. At this point, I will spread my fingers like a rake and lightly go down the muscle in-between the ribs (Intercostals) feeling for tension in the ribcage. Tension in the ribcage can cause poor performance because the horse will be having trouble taking deep breaths. Horses can't run or perform if they can't breath well. Now that you have completed the back and barrel, mentally add any other areas of tightness or tension to your body map.

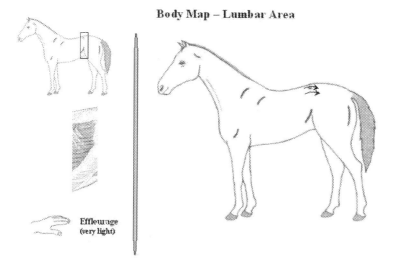

Body Map – Lumbar Area

Effleurage
(very light)

From here I move on to the lower-back area, the Lumbar region. This area is the vertebral region just in front of the Tuber Coxae (point of the hip) and Tuber Sacrale (point of the croup). Most working horses will have some tension in this area. As you glide your fingers down the back toward the rump, you might feel denseness, almost stopping your fingers as they glide to the rump. Make a mental note of the size of the tightness and congestion in this area. The body tells a story, weather it's a rider posting too hard, improper saddle fit, or a horse that isn't being supported properly by its anatomy. Horses with long backs can carry a lot of tension in this area. Regardless of the cause, it's your job to work out the tension and help your horse have a healthy back. Add the size and depth of the tension to your body map.

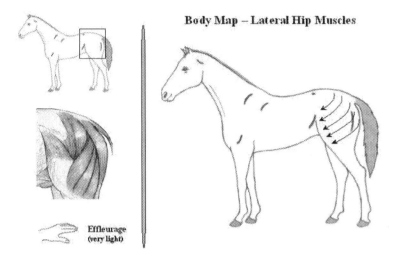

Body Map – Lateral Hip Muscles

Effleurage (very light)

I now make long sweeping strokes from the top of the croup to the flank area, assessing the tone and quality of the lateral hip muscles. These muscles aid in propulsion, and may be tight in horses that climb hills, as in trail riding.

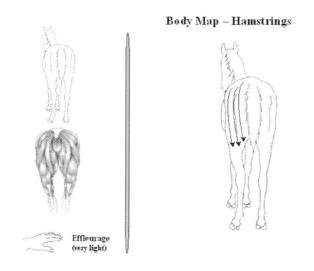

Body Map – Hamstrings

Effleurage
(very light)

Then I move to the side and slightly behind the
horse to place my hands at the top of the croup (Tuber
Sacrale) and glide down the posterior muscles all the
way to the hock. I'm checking again for any deviation
in tone, temperature, or quality of muscle. The muscles
of the hindquarters are 4 to 6 inches deep, and are used
for propulsion, rearing, and kicking. You may find
issues in this area especially in sport horses

Now do the same thing with the right side of the
horse. Once you have completed the right side of the
horse, you now have the information to mentally build
your picture of the horse's body issues – *The Body
Map.*

Incidentally, I use the same Effleurage stroke that I
used to build the body map to finish the full body
massage that we will be looking at in the next chapter.

87

This light stroke closes the horse's muscles and gives him an indication that the massage is ending.

Regardless of how many or how few issues I find while building this body map, I always give the horse a full-body massage, addressing every muscle. Massage is like peeling an onion – when one layer is removed the next layer is exposed. This means that when you release one muscle, another muscle's issues will surface. As a result, the body map you formed in the beginning is just a mental guide of where to start for a full-body massage. It may need to be refined as you work through the complete massage.

Chapter 11:

The One-Hour, Full-Body

Massage

Now that you have your "Body Map", you are ready to begin the actual massage. For continuity, let's start on the left side of the horse. You can use any of the massage strokes you have just learned in any combination that works for you. Throughout this chapter, I will be listing the strokes that have worked for me in each area of tension; but you should use whatever strokes feel right to you. A good massage touches every muscle in the horse's body. Areas that don't have issues can be stroked with a light Effleurage, while those that have issues require greater attention.

Each of the illustrations that follow will show the area of the horse's body that is being worked, the muscle structure of that area, the stroke that I use to massage that area, and a diagram of the flow of the hands when using that stroke.

Before we go into each specific area, it is important to realize that the massage must be kept *balanced and blended.* By this I mean doing a set of muscles first on one side and then on the other, rather than doing all the muscles on the left and then all the muscles on the right. If you have ever had someone scratch only one side of your back, you know what I mean; the other side is screaming to be scratched as well. Horses feel the same way when you massage their muscles. The following may be used as a guide to keep your massage balanced and blended.

To keep the massage balanced and blended, start with the left side of the neck, and then go to the right side and work on the neck there. While you are on the right side, do the right shoulder and right-front leg. Then move back to the left side and do the left shoulder and left-front leg. Next do the left upper back and barrel. Then go around to the horse's right side and massage his right upper back and barrel. Now stay on the right side and start working on glutes and work down the hindquarters and right-hind leg, stopping at the hock. Finally, go to the left side and massage the glutes, the hindquarters and left-hind leg, again stopping at the hock. This will complete the full-body massage in a balanced and blended manner.

You don't have to start your massage on the poll and neck, you can start anywhere; just remember to keep it balanced and blended. For some horses, starting the massage by the head is just too invasive. For those horses I start from the rear and work toward the head. For other horses, especially those on which I am doing rehab, I plan the massage to end at the 'worst" point last, so that the horse is totally relaxed when I get to his "uncomfortable" area. If I start with the worst area first, the horse doesn't relax during the massage and misses all the benefits. Additionally, by leaving the worst for last, the horse is so relaxed, that even that area is much easier to massage and the horse allows you to get in deeper and really release adhesions.

In the following sections, we will look at each area of the horse and discuss which strokes work best, with a description of exactly how to apply that stroke.

The Poll

The Poll area can get tight for many reasons. When working in a collected frame, the horse must bend at the poll causing tension. This can also be caused by the rider holding the reins too tightly. Also, the horse can overuse his poll by playing with other horses over the fence or in the paddock. Regardless of the reason, tightness in this area may cause your horse to hold his head low or tilt it off to one side. There are some wonderful ways to release the stress in this area.

Place your thumb and fingers across the mane and massage in little circles employing a Petrissage stroke, using the pads of your thumb and fingers to relax the muscles.

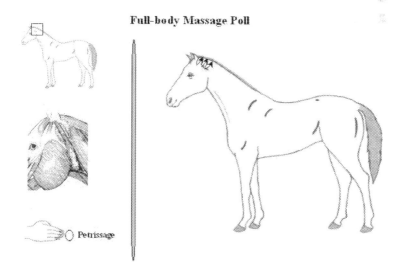

Full-body Massage Poll

Petrissage

91

Alternatively, you could use Petrissage to loosen the fascia and congested muscles on the Atlas. Take your fingertips and pull down in a straight line to the wing of the Atlas. Then use the side of your thumb, running it under the bony ridge of the Atlas to release muscle tension.

Full-body Massage Poll

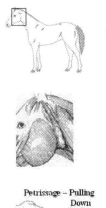

Petrissage – Pulling Down

The Neck

Properly functioning neck muscles are important, because if the neck is sore or stiff it can affect the way the horse moves (walks, trots, canters) and his ability to do both lateral and vertical flexion. Additionally, he will have difficulty walking in a straight line and can be off when doing circles.

Start by using long, smooth Effleurage strokes with the palm of your hand to warm the muscles of the neck. Make several passes, increasing the pressure a little with each pass. This will sufficiently warm the neck muscle. As the strokes get closer to the shoulder, let them run along the ridge in front of the shoulder and ending at the point of the shoulder.

Full-body Massage Neck

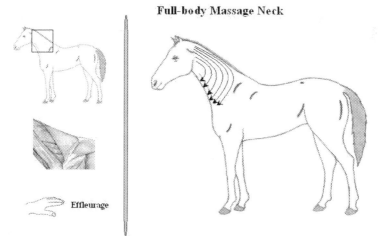

Effleurage

At this point, if there is still congested or tight areas in the neck, I would use a Friction stroke employing thumb bands across the grain of the muscle to restore tissue mobility and break down any adhesions in the muscle tissue.

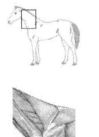

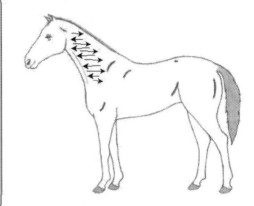

Full-body Massage Neck

Friction –
Thumb
Bands

Now cup your hand around the Brachiocephalicus, which is the long "row like" muscle in the lower neck that runs from under the jaw line to the point of the shoulder. Using a Petrissage stroke, do a light kneading and squeezing of the muscle all the way down to the shoulder. The hard, block-like things you feel in your hand are the Cervical Vertebras, so don't use too much pressure.

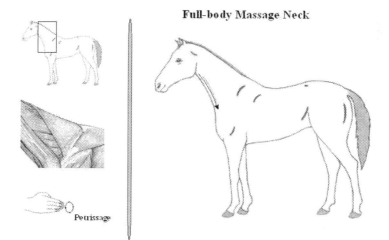

Full-body Massage Neck

Petrissage

Repeat the Poll and Neck massage on the right side of the horse.

The Chest – Pectoral Muscles

You are now standing on the right side of the horse, just having completed the poll and neck massage on the right, so begin the Pectoral massage from there.

The Pectoral muscles will feel different in almost every horse. Some horses will be very fit and the Pectoral's will feel very tight and stringy, similar to the muscles of a human runner's calf. Others will have very mushy Pectoral's because they haven't been exercised very much. And yet other Pectoral muscles will feel nice, full, and firm; these are the muscles of a conditioned horse. Difficulty in these muscles may make your horse have a shortened stride, or refuse to take the proper lead, or have girthing issues. Horses can display any combination of these symptoms when their Pectoral muscles are tight.

Face the body of your horse while standing at the right shoulder. Put your right hand around the front Pectoral muscle, centered in the middle by the inside of the leg. Put your left hand around the back of the leg, under where the girth runs. Now, bending your knees and lifting both hands simultaneously, pull your hands up by straightening your legs. Then bring your hands to the original position by simultaneously pushing your hands toward the girth area and bending your knees. It's your knee action that gives you the massage motion and pressure. This is an Effleurage stroke and should be repeated three times. The dotted line in the illustration indicates the motion of the hand that is behind the leg.

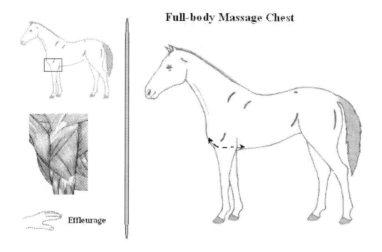

Full-body Massage Chest

Effleurage

Another option for massaging the Pectoral muscles is to do a firm kneading and vibration of the muscle. Warm the muscle first with an Effleurage stroke and then do a Petrissage stroke massaging the muscle until it is warm and pliable.

Repeat the Pectoral massage on the left side of the horse.

The Withers and Shoulder Area

Since you are standing on the left side of the horse after completing the Pectoral massage on the left side, start your Withers and Shoulder massage on the left. Remember that this side-to-side action keeps the massage balanced and blended.

The Withers and Shoulder areas are comprised of many muscles designed to move the shoulder forward and backward, while keeping the horse's barrel securely in place between the front legs.

The repetitive movements of any gait, and the stress of difficult maneuvers, like the impact of landing after a jump can cause stress and tension in this area. Muscle issues in these areas can lead to a non-specific loss of power, difficulty with coordination, shortened stride, problems performing lateral movements like side-passes, and decreased neck flexibility; all of these can mask as lameness in the front-end. Clearly, the withers and shoulder muscles need to remain functioning properly.

The Withers

Stand facing your horse on the left side at the Withers area. Run the pads of your fingers around the top of the Scapula, using an Effleurage stroke to warm the area above the Scapula. Repeat this stroking several times until you think the area is warm, and then use your fingertip pads to draw little circles from the top of the Withers around the top of the Scapula, moving in a semi-circular path to the end of the Withers. This is a Petrissage stroke designed to release tension between the vertebras of the Withers.

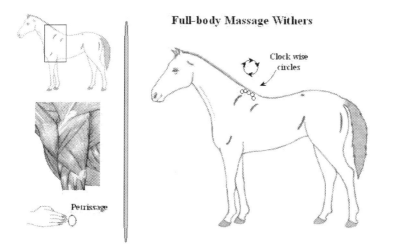

Full-body Massage Withers

Clock wise circles

Petrissage

If congestion is still present in the Withers, you could use a Friction stroke using thumb bands to break-up any adhesions, using a little more pressure than in the Petrissage stroke above. Start at the top of the Withers, place the tips of your thumbs facing each other, and draw them apart. Move about a half an inch following the same path around the top of the Scapula as before. Place the tips of your thumbs together, and draw them apart. Continue this until you are at the bottom of the Withers. Finish the area with an Effleurage stroke to smooth out the muscle.

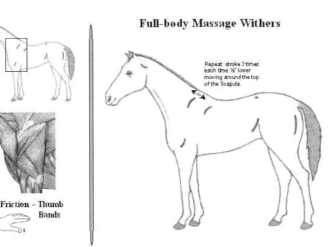

Full-body Massage Withers

Repeat stroke 3 times each time ½" lower moving around the top of the Scapula.

Friction – Thumb Bands

The Shoulder

Still standing on the left side of the horse, use an Effleurage stroke to open the muscles of the Shoulder. Starting at the top of the Withers, use a long smooth stroke to come down to the point of the shoulder and circle around the bottom of the Scapula, making sure you are not on top of the Scapular Spine. Then come up the shoulder circling around the top of the Scapula and come back down to the point of the shoulder. Repeat this three times. Do this all the way down to the point of the shoulder.

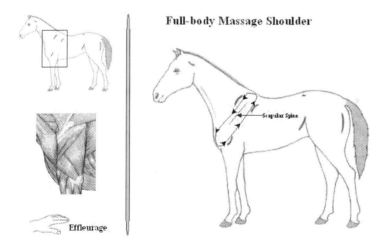

Full-body Massage Shoulder

Scapular Spine

Effleurage

If the shoulder still feels tight, you can use a Friction stroke across the muscle fibers to open the shoulder, Locate the Scapular Spine by running the flat palm of your hand horizontally across the middle of the shoulder blade. You will feel a hard ridge, like the edge of a cup, under your palm. Remember where it is and make sure that you are not pushing directly down on it in this stroke. You are going to use this Friction stroke to work the muscle on either side of the Scapular Spine.

Start at the top of the Withers with the muscle on the left side of the spine and place the pads of your fingers on the anterior edge of the Scapula (toward the horse's head) and push the muscle toward the Scapular Spine. Do this all the way down to the point of the shoulder.

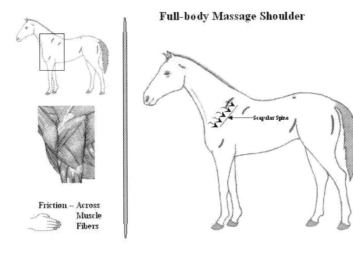

Friction – Across
Muscle
Fibers

Full-body Massage Shoulder

Scapular Spine

Now, start at the top of the Withers on the right side of the Spine, and place the pads of your fingers on the posterior edge of the Scapula (toward the horse's rump) and pull the muscle toward the Scapular Spine. Do this all the way down to the point of the shoulder.

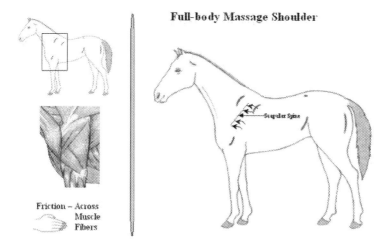

Full-body Massage Shoulder

Scapular Spine

Friction – Across Muscle Fibers

Next, do another Effleurage stroke to smooth out the muscle fibers. Continue this all the way down to the point of the shoulder and back up again.

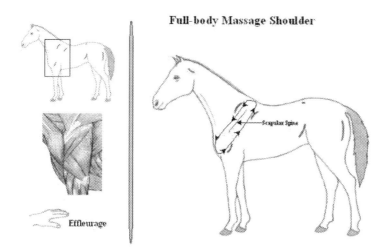

Full-body Massage Shoulder

Scapular Spine

Effleurage

Moving down the shoulder, we find the Triceps muscle, which is that "meaty" muscle at the top of the foreleg. Difficulty in this muscle can have your horse looking lame at the extended trot, may result in a shortened foreleg stride, or may cause your horse to avoid the proper lead when jumping. Using an Effleurage stroke, do smooth half circle strokes moving toward the elbow.

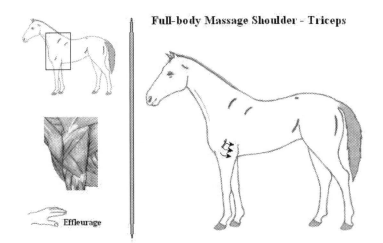

Full-body Massage Shoulder - Triceps

Effleurage

Alternatively, you could use a Petrissage stroke by firmly kneading and squeezing the muscle with your whole hand.

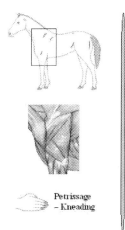

Full-body Massage Shoulder - Triceps

Petrissage – Kneading

Front Leg

The muscles of the foreleg are responsible for the action of the knee, the fetlock, and the hoof. If you have difficulties with these muscles, it can limit the extension of the hoof during protraction of the leg or limit the flexion of the hoof during retraction of the leg. Since these muscles run vertically from the top of the leg to insertion points on the Cannon and Pastern bones, they visually appear as little triangle-shaped muscles.

Use a Petrissage stroke to firmly knead the muscle around the fore arm all the way to the inside of the leg. Do this stroke for both the front and back part of the leg. Only massage down to the knee, since there are no muscles, only ligaments and tendons, below the knee.

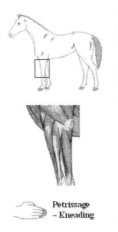

Petrissage
– Kneading

Full-body Massage Front Leg

Alternatively, you could use a Friction stroke employing thumb bands to go across the grain of the muscle to restore tissue mobility and break down any adhesions in the muscle tissue.

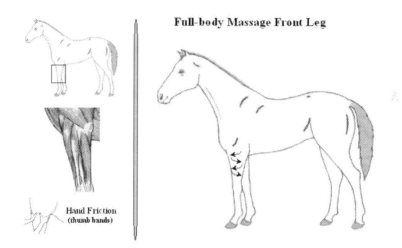

Full-body Massage Front Leg

Hand Friction
(thumb bands)

Additionally, you could use a firm Effleurage stroke to trace down the muscle from the top of the foreleg to the knee.

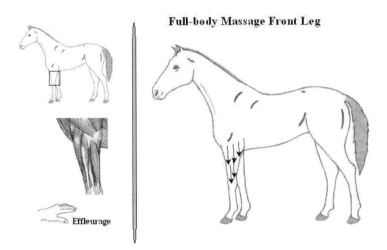

Full-body Massage Front Leg

Effleurage

Repeat the Withers, Shoulder, and Foreleg massage on the right side of the horse.

Since you are standing on the right side of the horse, you will now progress the massage forward along the horse's body by massaging the back and ribcage on the right side of the horse. (Another example of balancing and blending the massage.)

The Back

The longest muscle in the horse's body is the Longissmus Dorsi and it runs from the Withers to the Croup. It is responsible for extension of the back and lateral movement of the spine. This muscle group of the back prevents the back from sagging, stabilizes the ribcage, and causes lateral flexion and bending.

When injured, horses will have back pain, loss of coordinated power while in motion, often act like they are "Cold Backed", and have difficulty with lateral bending. The jarring that jumping horses sometimes experience upon landing is an example of how this muscle gets injured. Among the many other causes of back pain is poor saddle and pad fit.

There are many ways to approach a back massage; but one of the best ways for me is to face the horse (standing on the horse's right side), starting at the withers with a light Effleurage stroke. Place your hands just shy of the spine, using the pads of your fingers, and pull the muscle down toward the ground, until your hand encounters the rib shelf which is about four to six inches from the spine. Continue this movement all the way to the Croup. Make two more passes identical to the first, but using firmer pressure.

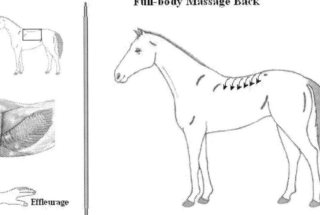

Full-body Massage Back

Effleurage

Then smooth the back muscle by using a light Effleurage stroke starting at the Withers, running perpendicular to the ground, all the way back to the Croup. Repeat this stroke one or two more times depending on how the muscle feels. If it is still congested, repeat it again.

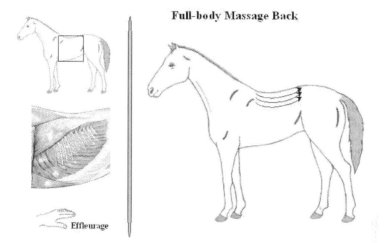

Full-body Massage Back

Effleurage

An alternative to the Effleurage stroke described above is a Compression stroke to open the back and break down any adhesions. Start by facing the horse with your hand at the withers, fingers touching the spine, but not pressing on it. Use the spine only as a guide for your hands to follow since putting pressure on the spine could bruise the muscle. Then begin smooth, half-circle pumping strokes with the heal of the hand, moving toward the hip, until you reach the Croup. Repeat this two more times, each time moving about one inch down toward the ribcage. This increases circulation and reduces back stress.

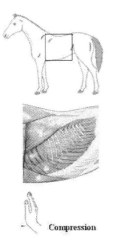

Compression

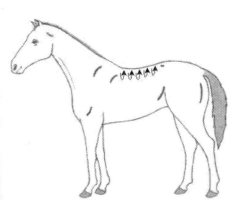

Full-body Massage Back

The Ribcage

The muscles located between the ribs, the Intercostal muscles, are responsible for inspiration (breathing in) and expiration (breathing out). When these muscles are tight or under stress, the horse has trouble breathing, and is unable to achieve maximum performance. Horses that are girthed too tightly often display shallow breathing because they are unable get expansion of the ribs. The Abdominal Oblique muscles are responsible for lateral bending of the ribcage and rounding of the back. If there are difficulties in these muscles, the horse will have restricted lateral bending and difficulty working in a collected frame.

Starting at the back of the withers, stack your hands, one on top of the other, using the flat of your hand, and drawing them down to the girth area. This is also an Effleurage stroke, so it should be long and smooth using light pressure for the first pass, and increasing the pressure as you repeat the stroke. Repeat this three times. This lengthens the muscle fibers in the girth area and will make the horse more comfortable during saddling.

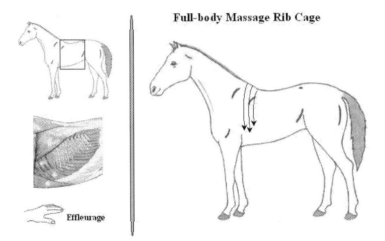

Full-body Massage Rib Cage

Effleurage

Next massage the ribcage by making a "rake" shape with your hand. Start at the last rib, just before the flank area, since it is the easiest one to find, and place it between two of your fingers. Draw the fingers down the side of the belly of horse. Move your hands back up and over to the next rib going toward the front of the horse. Repeat the downward stroke toward the belly. Continue moving to the next rib and pulling down until you can no longer feel any ribs, due to the muscle layers covering them. Repeat this whole process until you no longer feel tension in the muscles.

This will release the Intercostal muscles and help your horse breath. A variation on the above is to vibrate your fingers as you rake down the ribs.

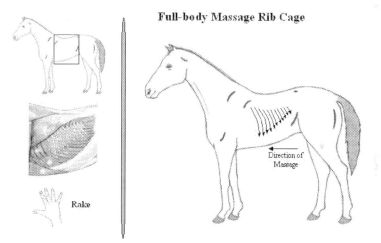

Full-body Massage Rib Cage

Rake

Direction of Massage

Now go to the Left side of the horse and repeat the Back and Ribcage massage.

The Hindquarters

The hindquarters are the "drive train" of the horse. They are made up of the Gluteus muscles (movers of the hip), the Hamstrings (power muscles), and the hind leg muscles. The combination of these muscles provide propulsion and speed, and the ability to rear and kick. When these muscles are having difficulties your horse may show lameness, shortened stride, loss of power, and scuffing of the hind feet. Additionally, if there is tightness between the lower-back muscles and the Gluteus muscles, the horse will have back pain.

The Gluteus Muscles

The gluteus muscles and the back muscles have a special relationship. These muscles are involved in forward motion (protraction), and both must be released, free of tension and adhesions, for the hindquarters to operate properly. If you release only the Loin area and not the Glutes, the back will still have issues, and vice versa. As a result, if your horse is showing either back or hindquarter pain and you only release one area, the problem will persist. The Gluteus muscles are four to six inches thick, so you can use firm pressure without fear of bruising the horse.

Standing back by the left side of the horse's rear end, place the flat of your hands on the lower-back (Loin) area and make a long smooth stroke, pulling your hands along the lower-back, and flowing down the back of the butt all the way to the hock. This is a Effleurage stroke and should be repeated three times.

Full-body Massage Gluteus

Effleurage

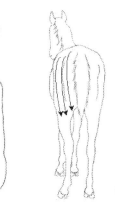

Next, stand facing the horse's left hindquarters by the flank, and place the flat of your hand up by the spine making long smooth semi-circle strokes toward the flank. Repeat this movement all the way down to the top of the hind leg Repeat this series of strokes three times. With this stroke you are massaging both the Superficial Glute as well as one of the Hamstrings, the Biceps Femoris.

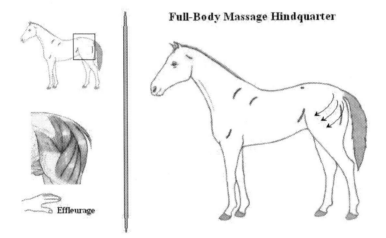

Full-Body Massage Hindquarter

Effleurage

The Hamstrings

Stand back by the horse's tail at the rear of the horse, placing your right hand with fingers by the tail. Make smooth half circle strokes on the hamstrings moving away from the tail toward you. Repeat this Friction stroke, all the way down to the hock.

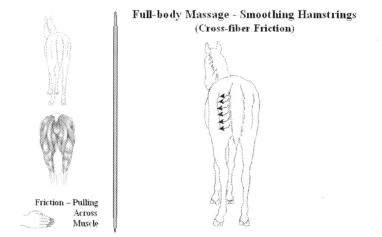

Friction – Pulling
Across
Muscle

Full-body Massage - Smoothing Hamstrings
(Cross-fiber Friction)

Still standing on the left side of the horse by the rear end, place the flat of your hand on the top of the Croup and make long smooth strokes coming down the hindquarters to the hock. We are using this Effleurage stroke to smooth down the muscle fibers previously spread out by the Friction stroke. Repeat this Effleurage stroke three times, using a little more pressure on each pass.

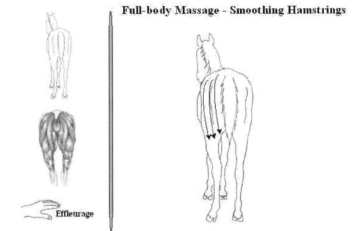

Full-body Massage - Smoothing Hamstrings

Effleurage

120

The Hind Leg

The Gaskin muscles are the big "hunkie" muscles surrounding the top of the hind leg. When the horse has difficulty in these muscles, he will hold his leg loose (flexed) and will show discomfort when standing. During movement, the horse may show lameness in the hind leg and restricted forward motion.

Use a Petrissage stroke to firmly knead the muscle around the hind leg toward the inside of the leg. Do this stroke for both the front and back part of the leg. You only have to go down to the hock, because there aren't any muscles below the hock, only ligaments and tendons.

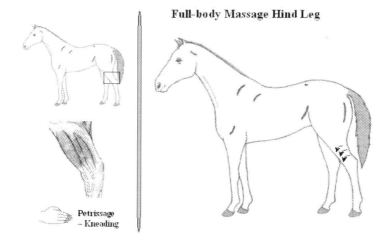

Full-body Massage Hind Leg

Petrissage
– Kneading

Or you could use a Friction stroke, employing thumb bands to go across the grain of the muscle to restore tissue mobility and break down any adhesions in the muscle tissue.

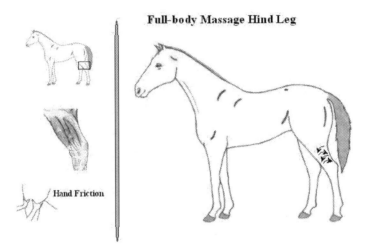

Full-body Massage Hind Leg

Hand Friction

Repeat the Hindquarters and Hind Leg massage on the right side of the horse.

A Final Effleurage

The last step is to close the horse's body by doing a very light, quick Effleurage stroke on each side working from the neck to the shoulders, front leg, the back, ribcage, hindquarters, and hind leg. Make one complete pass on each side of the horse, in contrast to the balancing and blending that was done during the main massage. This also lets the horse know that the massage has concluded.

To get maximum benefit from your massage, the horse should have 24 hours of rest. If this is impractical, he should have at least an overnight rest period. You may put your horse out where he can walk and roll, or you may want to put him in his stall to rest for the night. When a horse rolls, he is doing self-adjustment of his frame, so don't be surprised if he rolls after his massage. The massage has lengthened the muscle fibers in his body, allowing him to do this self-adjustment.

See Appendix D for a table of "Muscle Issues by Area" which summarizes the various areas of the horse where muscle tension might occur, their possible causes, the signs by which you can recognize them, and the strokes you can use to release the tension in these areas.

Chapter 12:

Massage For Specific Areas

In the last chapter we described how you will perform a full-body massage. However, certain activities that the horse may participate in may cause additional stress to specific areas and muscles. In this chapter, we will look at these specific activities, the problems that they can cause, and how to address them. Recognizing these can allow you to concentrate more on these areas during the full-body massage, or to provide additional comfort by massaging these areas between full-body massages.

Understanding the specific areas of stress for the horse and rider while competing in a specific discipline will allow you to be proactive in providing for the muscle needs of both you and your horse. While reading through this section, you will notice that your body and your horse's body "mirror" each other in muscle tension. Have you heard the old saying "Your horse's body mirrors your body's ailments"? It is true. If you are having trouble with a hip or some other part of your body, more than likely your horse is having issues in that same area. The reason for this is that your hip trouble may cause you to favor your other hip, causing more pressure on that side on the horse's back. Throughout this chapter, we will see examples of this "horse and rider connection" between your issues and his. For each discipline, we will first look at the issues that that discipline can cause in the horse, and then at the corresponding issues that the rider may experience.

Use the illustrations in this chapter of the specific areas in your horse that can be affected by the various disciplines to identify those muscles on which you should concentrate during the full-body massage.

The horse's body tells a story of how it has been used in various disciplines. This section is a compilation of "body issues" that I have addressed in horses over the past 10 years. The horse's body can show the strength of the rider, the training effects on muscles and frame, and the horse's overall body condition. For example, horses who have been working on "self-carriage" will have stronger back muscles, better posture, and better balance than a pasture pony. You can use this section as a guide for recognizing possible muscle tension and soreness in your horse.

The rider portion of this section is based on what horse owners have told me about their bodies' muscle tension and fatigue, as well as my own observations about my body. I am not a human massage therapist, so I am merely making observations about what works for alleviating my muscle tension, tightness, and fatigue in these areas.

Make sure that you select a discipline that supports your horse's conformation. Too many times, we choose competitive activities that are not appropriate for the conformation of our horses. Dr. Nancy Loving has written a great book on conformation and performance which shows us how conformation effects the activities and training of our horses. This is an excellent book for understanding equine conformation, performance consequences, training strategies, and selecting the best activity for specific types of horses. (See the appendix for a complete reference to this book.)

As an example of how the horse's conformation may affect his ability to compete in various disciplines, a horse with straight, upright, or vertical shoulders will have a shortened, rough, choppy stride. As a result, he will have a harder time elevating his shoulders and tightly folding his front legs, and may be less suitable for jumping.

Trail Riding

The first discipline we will look at is trail or pleasure riding. Trail riding can cause discomfort in a horse's back. The discomfort will start at the poll and run all the way back to and including the lower-back (Lumbar) area. Common causes for back discomfort include, but are not limited to, the following conditions. Perhaps the horse wasn't prepared for this type of activity, or maybe he had inadequate muscle preparation for the ups and downs of the trail. Additionally his saddle may not be fitting properly. At any rate, his back may be tired and a little sore after the ride. His natural way to "self-adjust" his back is to roll. Rolling allows for minor adjustments of the vertebrae and their facet joints, releasing the stress in the top-line. As a child, we always had a sandy spot in the corral for our horses to roll in after we rode. My father always made sure that there was plenty of room for them to roll and turn over without getting caught in the fence and casting themselves.

Massaging the entire top line, from poll to sacrum, will help relieve the stress and make his back feel better. Pay special attention to the horse's "Loin" (lower-back) area.

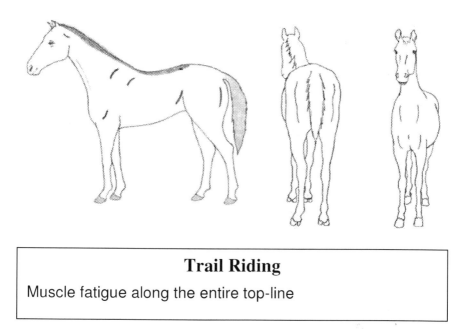

Trail Riding
Muscle fatigue along the entire top-line

You can also do belly lift stretches and Lumbar pushes to help eliminate the stress prior to riding. To perform the belly lift, stand facing the horse near the

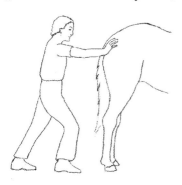

girth area, place your hands under his belly and, using your fingers, scratch his center midline while pushing up, moving toward his genitals. This will cause him to raise his top line. This should be followed by a Lumbar push which is good for the

Abdominal muscles, stretches the Gluteals and strengthens the back. Examples of massage strokes that release back tension effectively include Effleurage and Compression.

Trail riding can also cause aches in the lower back of the rider as well. Have you ever come home from a ride and gotten off and had your lower-back hurt? You can actually help this situation by self-massaging your lower back. I sometimes use a towel rolled into thirds and placed around my back as if I were going to tie it in front. I hold each end and lean into the towel and move it from left to right (side to side) giving me a self-massage. If my back is very tight, I do a pummeling massage stroke where I make light fists and gently strike my back to relieve the stress.

Another way to relieve stress in your lower back muscles is to do the flexibility stretch. It also creates flexibility in your hamstrings and calves.

Dressage

Dressage is about coordinated movement with elegance and finesse. As such, it is very exhausting both mentally and physically. Depending on the level of achievement, it takes months or years of preparation to prepare the muscles for the balanced co-ordination of the four limbs. Dressage mandates static-muscle work for the axial skeleton and middle-range muscle work for the limbs (appendicular skeleton). Stresses placed upon the stifle and hock when making advanced moves are almost incalculable. The "Ring of Muscles" diagram in Appendix B will give you an idea of the range of bones and muscles that are affected when the horse is required to work in a collected frame.

Because of this, the dressage horse will have muscle tension in his poll, along the jaw line, down his mid-neck muscles, down his forearms and medial muscles, along the entire top-line of the back, down his hindquarters (hamstrings) and Gaskin muscles (thighs) including medial muscles. Use a combination of massage strokes (Effleurage, Petrissage, Compression, and Friction strokes) to relieve these specific muscle issues.

Dressage: Collected Frame

"Coordinated Movement with Elegance and Finesse"
Muscle fatigue throughout the entire body.

Since there is so much going on with the horse's muscles from dressage, you will want to do all five equine stretches described in Chapter 5.

Dressage is also hard on the rider. The upper back, shoulders and base of the neck muscles will experience muscle fatigue and tightness. Additionally, the lower back, front of the thighs and the outside of the lower-legs feel stress and tightness from riding with deep heels and having to maintain posture and balance

Use the towel-massage described above for your shoulders and lower back. You can knead and squeeze the muscles of your thighs and lower legs to release the stress and tightness. Since there is also so much human muscle tension from dressage, you should do all five human stretches described in Chapter 5.

Endurance

Endurance riding is demanding on both horse and rider. Since it is a timed event, over many miles, it is necessary to do a considerable amount of trotting over varied terrain. As such, it stresses the back from the withers to the loins. Shoulder muscles, hamstrings and gaskin muscles are used for all the up and down hill work. Massaging the back from the withers all the way down the back to the hock will release the tension build-up. Special attention should be taken to massage the shoulder muscles and inner thigh of the hind leg.

Endurance

Timed Event, Varied terrain, Hill Work
Muscle fatigue is found in the Back (withers to loin),
Shoulders, Hindquarters

Again, referring to the stretches in Chapter 5, you will want to do the Hip Flexor and Stifle Extension to loosen the hind quarters, the Shoulder Rotation to relax the front end and help with lateral flexion and breathing, the Lumbar Push for loosening the abdominal muscles, and the Shoulder Extension to loosen the muscles and ligaments of the shoulder. The more difficult the activity, the more massage stroke combinations are required to release these muscle issues. An endurance horse definitely is deserving of a full-body massage!

For the rider, endurance riding causes stress to the lower back, front and inside of the thigh, as well as the calf muscles. Use the towel-massage described earlier in this chapter to release tension in the lower back. Rub the thigh and calf muscles, shaking them to relax. Follow this with the illustrated hamstring and calf muscle stretches to release the tension in these muscles.

Jumping

Jumping demands agility, balance, control and power from your horse. It takes a true equine athlete to clear the height and the spread of obstacles. Horse's tendons and muscles have to have extraordinary strength. The effort to rebalance during jumping and the jarring upon landing can torque the back muscles. A common problem is dislocation of the sacroiliac joint in a jumper who leaps over hurdles, causing what is known as a "Hunter's Bump". Additionally, the horse can exhibit sore knees from the strain of landing.

The stretches to use for a jumper are the Shoulder Rotation, the Lumbar Push, and the Lateral Neck Stretch described in chapter 5. Use a combination of massage strokes to address muscle issues in a horse used for jumping.

Jumping

Required elements are agility, balance, control, and power.
Muscle and tendon fatigue are common.
A full-body massage will do wonders.

A good general body massage, like the one-hour massage described in this book, will do wonders for your horse. It would be even better if you could do the massage before and after the jumping competition.

For the rider, jumping demands that you continually rearrange your body to take weight off of the horse's back, causing stress in your hips, knees, shoulders, and lower back. Use the towel massage described earlier in this chapter to rub your lower back. Use effleurage strokes and kneading and squeezing to rub the fronts of your thighs.

The stretches for the rider after jumping are the Hamstring and Calf Flexibility Stretch, Hip Flexor Stretch, and the Gluteus Stretch described in Chapter 5.

The Sport Horse

Sport-horse games of Barrel Racing, Polo, Cutting, and Reining place huge demands on the horse's body. They require acceleration, deceleration, turns, and extreme efforts to maintain balance.

Barrel racing requires fast starts, tight turns, extreme acceleration and then a hard stop at the end. Polo demands acceleration, deceleration, and fast turns that all require extreme efforts to maintain balance. In cutting, tremendous torque is put on the front legs and shoulders to provide the constant changing of direction required to respond to the cow's every move. The reigning horse must come to a sliding stop, and then perform a series of spinning turns.

These sports place ever-increasing demands on our horses. Consequently, they have soreness and tension in their necks, shoulders, legs, backs, and hindquarters.

Sport Horse

Required elements are agility, balance, control, and power:
Fast starts, tight turns, extreme acceleration, and hard
stops.
Muscle and tendon fatigue are common.
A full-body massage will do wonders.

Because of the affect of these requirements on the horse's muscles, all five equine stretches described in Chapter 5 are called for. A general, full-body massage will do wonders for these athletes.

For the rider, demands are placed upon the neck and shoulders, lower back, thighs and calves. Use the towel-massage described earlier in this chapter for your shoulders and lower back. You can knead and squeeze the muscles of your thighs and lower legs to release the stress and tightness.

The appropriate stretches for the rider are the Chest and Shoulder Stretch, Hamstring and Calf Flexibility Stretch, Hip Flexor Stretch, and the Gluteus Stretch described in Chapter 5.

Racing horses as a sport has been popular for hundreds of years. I'm leaving out racing as a specific area because, in my opinion, racing horses as two-year olds is detrimental to their health and body. The fusion of their growth plates has not completed, causing them to be susceptible to catastrophic injury.

Growth Plate Fusion

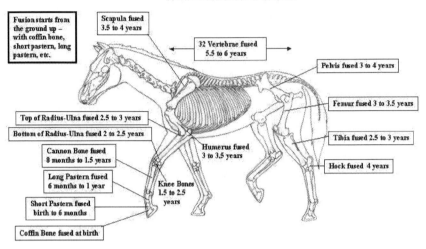

Fusion starts from the ground up – with coffin bone, short pastern, long pastern, etc.

Scapula fused 3.5 to 4 years

32 Vertebrae fused 5.5 to 6 years

Pelvis fused 3 to 4 years

Femur fused 3 to 3.5 years

Top of Radius-Ulna fused 2.5 to 3 years

Bottom of Radius-Ulna fused 2 to 2.5 years

Tibia fused 2.5 to 3 years

Cannon Bone fused 8 months to 1.5 years

Humerus fused 3 to 3.5 years

Hock fused 4 years

Long Pastern fused 6 months to 1 year

Knee Bones 1.5 to 2.5 years

Short Pastern fused birth to 6 months

Coffin Bone fused at birth

As you can see, major bones and joints are still growing and haven't fused when these horses are asked to race. Tremendous stress is placed on the hindquarters of a horse when breaking from the starting gate. Additionally, the horse's long bones (Radius, Cannon, Pastern, Femur, Tibia, and Hocks), muscles, and tendons are stressed to the maximum during a race.

In the following chapter I will talk about the benefits of giving you and your horse a special treat – a "Spa Day". This will help him maintain his skin, coat, and spirit; and it will help you relax, gain clarity, and nurture your soul.

Chapter 13:
Soothing Waters For Horse
And Rider

For Horse

After a day of riding, horses love to have the salt, dirt, and sweat rinsed out of their coats. Additionally, shampooing horses prior to competition and horse shows makes their coats glisten and shine. Be careful when using shampoo and conditioners; failing to get the products rinsed out of the skin properly can cause dry skin, flaking, and itching. It has been my experience that if my horse isn't completely dry when I turn him out, he will roll and become a mud ball. I have had success with bathing my horses with a tea tree oil-based shampoo, such as Healing Tree Private Reserve Tea Tree Shampoo.

After shampooing, I apply a leave-in conditioner and Vetrolin liniment (two tablespoons of each) mixed in a half-gallon bucket of warm water. This regimen has worked for me during show season. In addition, there are products to whiten white horses, keep black horses blacker, and make the copper color come out in the coat of chestnuts. There are many liniments, bracers, and products to release sore muscles. Everyone has their own favorite products, so find what you like using on your horse and stick with it. The market place is full of great products for bathing and relaxing your horse. At the end of the ride, be sure to give your horse a special treat by removing all the salt, dirt, and sweat from his coat. Even if it's only a sponge bath of the dirty areas, he will love you for taking such good care of him.

For Rider

When I get done riding, brushing, and massaging my horse, I'm ready for a relaxing soak in the tub. I would like to share a couple of baths that have brought me relaxation and have encouraged my success with horses; they also promote spiritual awareness for a true human/horse relationship.

Tranquility Bath

Give yourself the gift of tranquility by melting away stress and tension with this bath. It is very healing for overworked, tired, and stressed muscles from a joyful day of riding. It uses Lavender to calm the wild animal in us and bring about a state of peace. The other ingredient in this bath is Marjoram, which was used in Roman times to promote longevity.

- 5 drops of Marjoram oil (Marjoram is a sedative and can cause drowsiness and should not be overused. It also should not be used by pregnant women.)

- 10 drops of Lavender oil (Lavender was used by the Greeks and Romans to reduce stress, high blood pressure, and cure insomnia.)

Pour the ingredients into a hot bath tub. Swirl the mixture around the tub. Soak in the bath for 20 minutes. Quiet your mind by concentrating on your breathing; focus on inhaling and exhaling. Pay attention to your heartbeat and its replenishing of your body's energy. Mentally relax the rest of your body and banish all stress.

Success Bath

This second bath is for increasing your aptitude for success.   If you are having trouble achieving the success you want with your horse, try this bath to remove blocks to the success you desire. Lavender releases emotional conflicts that are blocking your growth, and Lemon promotes mental clarity.

- 10 drops Lavender oil
- 10 drops Lemon oil

Visualize the things that have been blocking you being loosened from around your heart and solar plexus area. Swish the water around you and feel the blocks dissolving. Soak in the bath for 30 minutes. I sometimes stay in longer if I feel like my body is continuing to release all the roadblocks to my success. Rinse with warm water after the bath to physically cleanse the released blocks from your body.

Chapter 14:

In Closing

By opening your mind and clearing your thoughts, building your strength so you can became a strong rider, and increasing the flexibility and health of your horse, you will become more successful in every endeavor you challenge as a team. Massage will help you develop the multi-level connection that will deepen and strengthen your relationship with your horse. By doing these things, you will make your equine companions healthier, keep them happier and performing better. You can do all of the things I have shared with you in this book to make living with horses more pleasurable and rewarding. I sincerely hope that you enjoy the journey to a multi-level connection as much as I have.

For me, horses are powerful beings. They lead me on a journey into my heart to find my true self; no walls, no facades, just me! Horses live in the moment and love us with all they have to give; they have brought me friendship and companionship without judgment – *Unconditional Love.*

Today, I want you to think about how you can be more compassionate with your horse. What if you had only one minute left in the world to tell your horse what he means to you; what would you say? If your horse is under distress by being ill or suffering from the loss of a companion horse, what do you think he would like to hear to give him comfort? Are there things you would like to apologize for. When I had Shadow branded, I had no idea what damage it would do to his fascia. It left it with adhesions so that skin and muscle movement are restricted. Have you told your horse how much he contributed to the joy in your life?

It takes this mental shift of compassion to truly develop a human/horse relationship.

It has been said that you can tell the true "timber" of a person by how he treats animals. Your choice is to "harm" or to "nurture" the animal and his spirit. I hope Equine Muscle Magic helps you create a more loving relationship with all the animals in your life.

Appendix A – Equine Muscle Chart

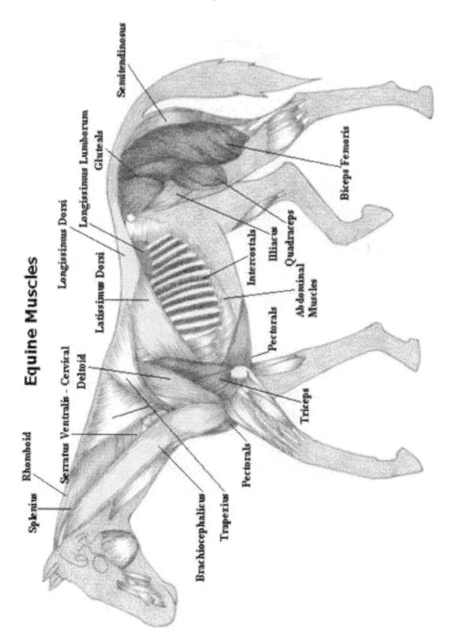

Equine Muscles

Appendix B – Ring of Muscles

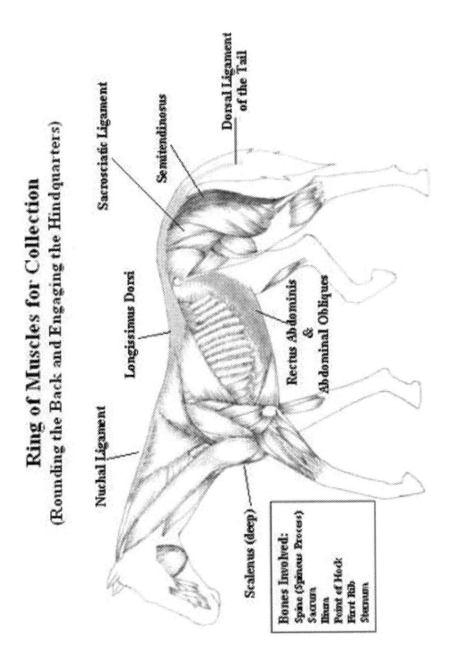

Ring of Muscles for Collection
(Rounding the Back and Engaging the Hindquarters)

Sacrosciatic Ligament

Semitendinosus

Dorsal Ligament of the Tail

Longissimus Dorsi

Rectus Abdominis & Abdominal Obliques

Nuchal Ligament

Scalenus (deep)

Bones Involved:
Spine (Spinous Process)
Sacrum
Ilium
Point of Hock
First Rib
Sternum

Appendix C – Muscle Pronunciation Table

As horse owners, we talk with many professional equine practitioners, such as veterinarians, farriers, and therapists. It is useful to be able to pronounce the terms we use correctly. This list is not all-inclusive, but rather, a listing of terms that may be new to you. Refer to Appendix E – Bony Landmarks a for graphic of the skeleton and bones, and Appendix A – Equine Muscles for a graphic of the superficial muscles. These graphics are limited to listing information that is specifically designed for beginning massage.

Skeleton	Appendicular skeleton - (ap-pen-dik-u-lar) Axial skeleton – (ak-see-ul)
Vertebrae	Cervical – (ser-vik-ul) Sacral – (say-crul) Thoracic – (tho-ra-sik)
Bones	Ishii – (ish-ee-i) Nuchal Crest – (new-k'l) Olecranon – (o-lek-rah-non) Trochanter – (tro-can-ter) Tuber – (too-burr) Tuber Calcis – (cal-sis)
Superficial Muscles	Biceps Femoris – (by-seps fem-or-iss) Brachiocephalicus – (bray-key-o-sih-fal-ik-us) Deltoid – (del-toyd) Gluteal – (glu-tee-ul) Intercostals – (in-ter-cos-tuls) Latissimus Dorsi – (lat-is-sim-us dor-sigh) Longissimus Dorsi – (lon-gis-sim-us dor-sigh) Serratus Ventralis – (sir-rat-us ven-tral-iss) Splenius – (spleen-ee-us) Triceps – (try-seps)

Appendix D – Muscle Issues by Area

(A few indicators not an all inclusive list)

(All persisting issues should be diagnosed by a Vet)

Poll Area	
Possible Cause	Working in a collected frame Holding reins too tightly Playing with other horses Knocking head on something
Signs	Holding head low Tilting head to one side Difficulty with lateral flexion of head and neck
Strokes	Petrissage – little circles Petrissage – pulling down Petrissage – side of thumb Compression – pumping of mane between fingers and palm of hand
Neck Area	
Possible Cause	Drilling in circles Pivots Over flexing neck (training or in play) Too much vertical flexion
Signs	Difficulty when doing lateral and vertical flexion Difficulty walking in a straight line Off when doing circles
Strokes	Effleurage – long, smooth strokes Friction – thumb bands Petrissage – light kneading
Chest Area (Pectorals)	
Possible Cause	Hill work Working in collected frame Jumping Pulling draft (heavy things)
Signs	Shortened stride Refusal or difficulty taking proper lead

	Girthing issues
Strokes	Effleurage – long, smooth strokes Petrissage – firm kneading

Withers Area

Possible Cause	Repetitive movements Jumping impact Poor tack fit
Signs	Non-specific loss of power Difficulty in coordination Shortened stride Problems performing lateral movements Front-end lameness Decreased neck flexibility
Strokes	Effleurage – long, smooth strokes Friction – thumb bands Petrissage – small circles

Shoulders Area

Possible Cause	Repetitive movements Jumping impact Poor tack fit
Signs	Non-specific loss of power Difficulty in coordination Shortened stride Problems performing lateral movements Front-end lameness Decreased neck flexibility
Strokes	Effleurage – long, smooth strokes Friction – pulling and pushing muscles entire length of scapula

Triceps Area

Possible Cause	Repetitive movements Jumping impact
Signs	Lame at extended trot Shortened foreleg stride Avoiding proper lead when jumping

Strokes	Effleurage – long, smooth ½ circles Petrissage – firm kneading
Front Leg Area	
Possible Cause	Running (speed) Repetitive movements Jumping
Signs	Limited extension of hoof during protraction of leg Limited flexion of hoof during retraction of leg
Strokes	Petrissage – firm kneading around leg Friction – thumb bands across grain of muscle Effleurage – long, smooth strokes tracing down the muscle
Back Area	
Possible Cause	Long back Jarring impact of jumping Poor tack fit Impact of posting trot
Signs	Back pain Loss of coordinated power Cold Backed Difficulty with lateral bending
Strokes	Effleurage – pull down movement to rib shelf Effleurage – long, smooth strokes along entire back Compression – ½ circles toward spine
Ribcage Area	
Possible Cause	Girthed too tightly Overworked in collected frame Kicked by another horse
Signs	Trouble breathing Difficulty achieving maximum performance Restricted lateral bending Difficulty working in collected frame
Strokes	Effleurage – long, smooth strokes using light

	pressure
	Raking – pulling down on muscle between ribs

Hindquarters Area	
Possible Cause	Overworked Hill work Fast starts
Signs	General lameness Shortened stride Loss of power Scuffing hind feet Back pain
Strokes	Effleurage – long, smooth strokes Friction – pulling across muscle fibers

Hind Leg Area	
Possible Cause	Drilling, repetitive movements Fast starts and stops Running Hill work
Signs	Holding leg loose (flexed) Discomfort when standing Lameness in hind leg when moving Restricted forward motion
Strokes	Petrissage – firm kneading Friction – thumb bands

Appendix E – Bony Landmarks

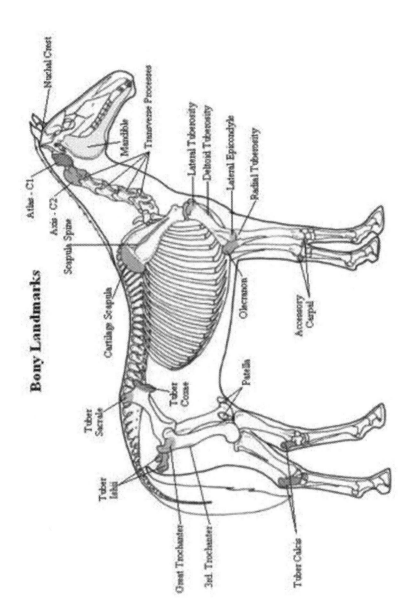

Appendix F – Parts of the Horse

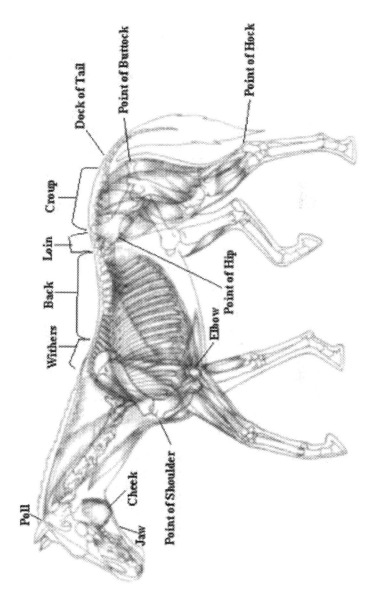

Points of the Horse

151

Appendix G – Bibliography

Biggs, Sharon, *Tack Fit*, HorseChannel.com, July 2007. http://www.horsechannel.com/horse-exclusives/horse-tack-fit.aspx

Bird, Catherine, *A Healthy Horse The Natural Way, The Horse Owner's Guide To Using Herbs, Massage, Homeopathy, and Other Natural Therapies*, Guilford, Connecticut, The Lyons Press, ISBN 1-58574-576-6

Blignault, Karin, *Stretch Exercises for your Horse – The Path to Perfect Suppleness*, North Pomfret, Vermont, Trafalgar Square Publishing, 2003.

Bromiley , Mary W., *Massage Techniques for Horse and Rider*, Marlborough, Wiltshire, UK, Crowood Press Ltd, 2002 (pp. 133-149).

Coates, Margrit, *Healing for Horses*, New York, Sterling Publishing Co., 2002. ISBN 0-8069-8963-7.

Coates, Margrit, *Horses Talking*, London, Ebery Press (Random House) 2005. ISBN 9781844131099.

Denoix, Jean-Marie, Jean-Pierre Pailloux, *Physical Therapy and Massage for the Horse*, North Pomfret, Vermont, Trafalgar Square Publishing, 1998.

Gandolfo, Justine, *How to Fit Your Western Bit*, October 2009, http://www.thehorse.com/Video.aspx?vID=299

Halstead, Doris Kay & Carrie Cameron, *Release the Potential – A Practical Guide to Myofascial Release for Horse & Rider*, Boonsboro, Maryland, Half Halt Press, Inc., 2000. ISBN: 0-939481-58-8.

Hannay, Pamela, *Shiatsu Therapy for Horses*, London, J.A. Allen (Robert Hale, Ltd.), 2002. ISBN: 0-84131-847-9.

Hourdebait, Jean-Pierre, R. M. T., *Equine Massage, A Practical Guide*, New York, Howell Book House (a Simon & Schuster Macmillan Company) 1997. ISBN 0-87605-998-1

Kamen, Daniel R., DC, *The Well Adjusted Horse*, Cambridge, Brookline Books, Inc., 1999. ISBN 1-57129-063-X

Loving, Nancy, DVM, *All Horse Systems GO*, North Pomfret, Vermont, Trafalgar Square Publishing, 2003. ISBN-10: 1-57076-332-1

Loving, Nancy, DVM, *Conformation and Performance*, Ossining, NY, Breakthrough Publications,1997. ISBN 914327-75-5

Lyons, John, "Get Fit and Ride Strong." *Perfect Horse* 12 [2] February 2007: 44-48.

Muryn, Mary, *Water Magic, Healing Bath Recipes for The Body, Spirit, and Soul*, New York, Simon & Schuster, 1995. ISBN 0-684-80142-6.

Snader, Meredith L., VMD, Sharon L. Willoughby, DVM, DC, Deva Kaur Khalsa, VMD, Craig Denega, Ihor John Basko, DVM., *Healing your Horse, Alternative Therapies*, New York, Macmillan General Reference, 1993. ISBN 0-87605-829-2.

Tellington-Jones, Linda & Ursula Bruns,*The Tellington-Jones Equine Awareness Method*, Millwood, NY, Breakthrough Publications, Inc, 1988. ISBN 0-914327-18-6